"*Sola Scriptura* is an admirably accessible work of fine scholarship. The book is well argued and constructed, lucidly written, and makes its case very well. It also takes on one of the most pressing issues in contemporary culture, namely the nature and location of authority. As always in his work, Ben Witherington ranges widely through a large and diverse literature, and he has an excellent familiarity with the more tangential literatures."

—PHILIP JENKINS, *Distinguished Professor of History, Baylor University*

"Dr. Witherington, as a seasoned scholar, presents a much-needed defense for the authority of Scripture with concise historical context for renewed significance for contemporary crises of faith untethered from the foundations of Scripture."

—M. SYDNEY PARK, *Associate Professor of Divinity, Beeson Divinity School*

"Questions about the canon, authority, and trustworthiness of the Bible are commonplace, even among Christians, and in *Sola Scriptura* Ben Witherington offers answers to those questions. He argues his thesis through his own historical summary and critical analysis of Jewish and Christian views on sacred texts, making the case that the Bible should be the final authority for Christian faith and practice today. This text is a gift to Christians who desire to ground their trust in the Bible with accessible historical evidence and offers much to ponder for Christians across the theological spectrum."

—HOLLY BEERS, *Associate Professor of Religious Studies, Westmont College*

"In this valuable volume, Ben Witherington III tackles a large topic—biblical authority. He does so insightfully and, for my part, convincingly. Tradition, reason, and experience notwithstanding, Witherington contends that sacred Scripture is the final and ultimate arbiter for matters of faith and practice. Whether or not you are inclined to embrace this theological position, you will benefit from reading this thoughtful and timely book, written by one of the foremost biblical commentators of our time."

—TODD D. STILL, *Charles J. and Eleanor McLerran DeLancey Dean & William M. Hinson Professor of Christian Scriptures, George W. Truett Theological Seminary at Baylor University*

Sola Scriptura

Scripture's Final Authority in the Modern World

Ben Witherington III

BAYLOR UNIVERSITY PRESS

Cover design by *the*BookDesigners.
Cover art courtesy of Shutterstock/Bogyofunk
Book design by Baylor University Press
Typeset by Scribe Inc.

Library of Congress Cataloging-in-Publication Data

Names: Witherington, Ben, III, 1951- author.
Title: Sola Scriptura : Scripture's final authority in the modern world / Ben Witherington III.
Description: Waco : Baylor University Press, 2023. | Includes bibliographical references and index. | Summary: "Chronicles the development of beliefs about Scripture's authority and the concept of Sola Scriptura to the present"-- Provided by publisher.
Identifiers: LCCN 2023025954 (print) | LCCN 2023025955 (ebook) | ISBN 9781481320467 (hardback) | ISBN 9781481320498 (adobe pdf) | ISBN 9781481320481 (epub)
Subjects: LCSH: Bible--Evidences, authority, etc. | Bible--History.
Classification: LCC BS480 .W575 2023 (print) | LCC BS480 (ebook) | DDC 220.1--dc23/eng/20230714
LC record available at https://lccn.loc.gov/2023025954
LC ebook record available at https://lccn.loc.gov/2023025955

You have studied the Holy Scriptures, which are true, and given by the Holy Spirit. You know that nothing unjust or counterfeit is written in them.

1 Clement 45:2–3

It is so impossible for divine inspiration to contain any error that, by its very nature, it not only excludes even the slightest error but must of necessity exclude it, just as God, the Supreme Truth, must also necessarily be absolutely incapable of promoting error. Consequently, any who were to admit that there might be error in the authentic pages of the sacred books . . . make[s] God himself the author of error.

Leo XIII, *Providentissimus Deus*

This study is dedicated to all my wonderful Bible and theology teachers over many years who have gone to be with the Lord in the last several decades—Bernard Boyd at UNC; David Scholer, Richard Lovelace, Meredith Kline, and now Gordon Fee at Gordon-Conwell; Bruce Metzger at Princeton; Krister Stendahl at Harvard; and C. K. Barrett, Charles Cranfield, John Rogerson, and T. H. L. Parker at the University of Durham. Without you I would never have become a New Testament scholar. Without you I would never have known how to be faithful to the Lord and to his Word while becoming the sort of scholar and teacher who does not fear dealing with the most difficult intellectual and historical challenges such a scholar faces all the time. They say you become what you admire. May the Lord bless you and keep you and make his face shine upon you and give you all his peace.

Ἐν ἀρχῇ ἦν ὁ Λόγος,

BW3

Contents

Preface

In a previous book entitled *The Living Word of God*, I explored at length issues involving the inspiration of the Scriptures, the canonizing of the Scriptures, and related matters. This study is not a repeat of that but rather focuses on one particular notion that has been applied to the Scriptures, particularly by Protestants ever since the German Reformation, namely that the Bible is the "sole" authority for the church and for Christian life. Interestingly, however, the Latin phrase *sola Scriptura*, as we shall see later in this study, was neither invented by Protestants, nor first applied to the Bible.

Furthermore, there is often a lack of clarity as to what is meant by the phrase—does it mean that the Bible is indeed the *only authority* or rule for faith and practice for the Christian, or does it mean the Bible is the *final authority*, allowing nonbiblical traditions, human reason, and perhaps even experience to have some authority in the church? The Bible could be the norm among norms, the final court of appeals in disputes if the phrase was meant to connote something other than "sole authority."

In the twentieth and twenty-first centuries, Evangelical Protestants have often been the most strident advocates for the notion that the Bible is the only real authority, the only real litmus test of truth and true Christian praxis for the church, but is this how early Jews and early Christians *who wrote the biblical books* viewed their sacred texts? And what counted as those sacred texts? I have shown in *The Living Word of God* that there was a concept of not merely inspired persons (e.g., prophets) but also of inspired texts. This is surely what 2 Tim 3.16 makes clear. There were God-breathed texts, and there were other texts that might convey some truths but were not divinely inspired.

So, let's go back to the time of the writing of the Bible and look at what is said about them, with a specific focus on how the authority of such texts was viewed, and then walk through Christian history until we get to point where the phrase *sola Scriptura* actually appears as an authority claim of some kind. Surprisingly, it doesn't show up until the fourteenth century A.D. and not in the writings of a Protestant. Thereafter, we will examine how the phrase continued to be used in the various Reformations and into the modern era.

But at the same time, we will need to examine the rise of science, the effect of the Enlightenment, and changes in views about human sexuality that have affected the discussion of *sola Scriptura* in various ways. One thing is for sure, this is an under-discussed subject, if by that we mean a subject studied across history and in various contexts. This study will *not* be exhaustive but illustrative of the process of the church trying to best understand the inspiration and authority of the Bible and their implications.

There are several good reasons such a study is needed not only by Bible students and budding scholars but also by pastors and laypeople at this juncture: (1) A profound historical amnesia is affecting even churches that are bibliocentric. They don't know the history of the Bible or the history of the struggle to affirm its final authority in Christian life. What exactly does the phrase "only Scripture" really mean, and what are its implications? As the saying goes, those who do not know or learn from the past are doomed to repeat its mistakes. (2) The general chaos in Western culture has just further alienated younger generations from the church and angered the older generations who still attend church, and very little of the discourse about our historical moment reckons seriously with the Bible's authority claims about what we should believe and how we should behave. The discussion is more fear driven than faith driven. (3) The increasing biblical illiteracy in the church, including in its pulpits, coupled with the increase in churches not requiring good graduate-level biblical education of their ministers, has led to churches taking their signals and sense of direction from the culture, including the political culture, not from the biblical witness itself. All of this reflects the crisis of authority in and for churches of all sorts. Such crises, particularly in Protestant churches, will not be overcome without a serious coming to grips with the Bible, its history, and its authority for faith and practice, for belief and behavior. I hope that this study can help us all do a better job of accepting and applying the biblical witness to ourselves and to an increasingly less Christian Western world.

Easter 2023

1

The People of the Book

Early Christian Appropriations and Additions

> Saturninius the proconsul said: "What are those things in your case?"
>
> Speratus replied: "Books and letters of Paul, a just man."[1]

Something besides monotheism set early Jews apart from their polytheistic religious environment, namely their being "the people of the Book," as they and Christians came to be called by Muslims later in religious history. Unlike ancient Near Eastern (ANE) and Greco-Roman religions, they had sacred texts they believed had come from God and by God's inspiration and were meant to be preserved as an ongoing source of inspiration, truth, and authority for the whole people of God.

It is interesting that the Hebrew phrase "the holy writings" first shows up in postbiblical writings, namely in the Mishnah (m. Shab. 16.1; Eruv. 10.3; Sanh. 10.6). However, the Greek equivalent to such a phrase is found earlier, already in Philo of Alexandria, who says, rather matter of factly, that the last chapter of Deuteronomy is "the end of the holy writings" (*Mos.* 2.290; or more generally see *Spec.* 2.159; *Praem.* 79; cf. *Opif.* 77).[2] Josephus' writings also bear witness to this concept of "Holy Writ," and Josephus is even prepared to speak about a certain number of books that count as Holy Writ (cf. *C. Ap.* 2.45; *Ant.* 3.38). Despite some recent views to the contrary, it appears reasonably clear that the Old Testament canon was viewed as a specific and basically closed collection of books not long after the destruction of the temple in Jerusalem in 70 A.D. *Indeed, it cannot be an accident that the only books the writers of the New Testament cite as Holy Writ are books from what we today call the thirty-nine books of the OT.*[3]

Not surprisingly, the repository of crucial documents was in temples throughout the ancient world. We do not need to doubt this was also the case already during the First Temple period in regard to the law of Moses. Note how the reforms of Josiah came about—2 Kgs 22 tells us that Hilkiah found the book of the law of Moses in the temple and read it to King Josiah. The same sort of practice surely existed during the Second Temple period, and as in the case of Josiah's reforms, the Scriptures were seen as having final authority as to what one should believe and what should be done. Josephus refers to this same event in *Ant.* 10.12–14 and to "the holy books of Moses deposited in the temple and found during Josiah's reign." He also mentions the actions of the prophet Samuel, who wrote the law of Saul's kingship and placed it in the sanctuary (1 Sam 10.25—*Ant.* 6.66).

Josephus speaks about what Samuel wrote as inspired texts that predicted the future of Saul's reign. Here we have the concept not merely of a sacred text but of an inspired text written by an inspired prophet. In *Ant.* 4.303 he says the same thing about the Song of Moses in Deut 32. C. T. R. Hayward concludes,

This evidence of Josephus suggests that not only the
books of Moses, but also prophetic and poetic parts of
scripture were preserved in the temple in his day. . . .
Elsewhere . . . (*Contra Apionem* 1.29) he states that the
Jews entrusted the keeping of their records to the high
priests and prophets; and he enumerates the twenty-
two books whose prophetic pedigree guarantees their
authenticity, noting how carefully they have been preserved (*Contra Apionem* 1.37–43). Prophets are those who
record tradition; and the temple appears to be the cen-
tre where records were kept, and where reference could
be made to them.[4]

What is perhaps most important about Hayward's helpful
discussion is that it reveals that it was not just any sort of
tradition that came to be considered Holy Writ in early
Judaism but inspired tradition, or as it was later put in
2 Tim 3.16, God-breathed tradition. This is a crucial point
for the ongoing discussion, for as we will see in early Christianity there were both Scripture and other valuable traditions, and already in the NT era Christian writings such
as Paul's letters were seen not merely as traditions but as
Scripture like the OT Scriptures.

However long the process of compiling the Law, the
Prophets (former and latter), and the Writings, abbreviated
as TANAK (Torah, Nevi'im, Ketuvim—cf. Jesus' reference
to the threefold division in Luke 24.44 and before that the
reference to "all the Scriptures" in Luke 24.27), by the NT
era there was wide agreement about a large corpus of sacred
writings that were to be seen as some sort of final authority
for the life of "the people of the Book." Clearly, it was not

seen as the only authority because particularly among the Pharisees there was also *halakah* and *haggadah*, traditions of interpretation of the Law and the biblical narrative that had some authority for believers, and in the community of Jesus' disciples there were also the new teachings of Jesus, as well as his interpretations of the Hebrew Scriptures. But there was eventually a difference in these two communities: namely the Pharisaic traditions never became a literal part of Holy Writ, whereas in due course the teachings of Jesus, Paul, Peter, James, Jude, and others did become part of a collection of sacred writings that were eventually called the New Testament.

Tertullian (155–220 A.D.) was not only the first person to use the term *trinitas*; he was apparently also the first person to apply the phrase "New Testament" to a collection of books by Christ's followers.[5] Prior to that, the earliest Christian (that we know of) to use the phrase "old covenant" of the Hebrew Scriptures is Paul (2 Cor 3.14). By the time of Tertullian, the terms "covenant" and "testament" were seen as basically synonymous, but Paul in the 50s A.D. is specifically referring to the Mosaic covenant.

What is obvious already in the earliest Christian documents, namely the letters of Paul, is that sacred texts were crucial to identity formation for Christians and the understanding of who they were. Gradually, this fact became obvious to outsiders, even to emperors, for by the time we get to Diocletian, a persecutor of Christians, his plan to stamp out what he viewed as a pernicious superstition involved confiscating and burning the texts so treasured by Christians in the empire. This transpired in February 303 A.D. But this action was too little and too late, because by the time Constantine became emperor shortly thereafter, the pendulum had swung almost completely in the other direction.[6]

As Margaret Mitchell rightly stresses, "An essential fact about early Christianity [is] it was a religious movement with texts at its very heart and soul, in its background and foreground. Its communities were characterised by a pervading, even obsessive preoccupation with and *habitus* for sacred literature. In the pre-Constantinian period, Christians succeeded in composing, collecting, distributing, interpreting and intimately incorporating a body of texts they found evocative enough to wish to live inside of."[7]

An understudied aspect of this whole process is the question—which Old Testament did the writers of the NT and later the church fathers see as Holy Writ? All of the writers of the NT wrote in Greek, and so it is not surprising that some, indeed perhaps the majority, used some Greek OT as their primary biblical source. That, however, means that the Bible *in translation* could be considered Scripture, even though the translation of the Septuagint (LXX) was far from literal in numerous places.

In a helpful article entitled "The Septuagint: The Bible of the Earliest Christians,"[8] Paul Lamarche makes clear that the Pentateuch of the LXX had already been translated by about 285 B.C., and the rest was completed in the first century B.C. at the latest. In other words, the LXX was readily available for NT writers to use by the time they began to write in the mid-first century A.D. Sometimes, the use was out of necessity (e.g., in the case of Luke, who seems to know no Aramaic and little if any Hebrew), but sometimes, as in the case of Paul, by choice, perhaps mainly because he was addressing a Greek-speaking audience. There is no trace of evidence that any of these NT writers hesitated to use the LXX because it was a translation.

As Lamarche points out, "Ordinarily Jewish authors, in using the Septuagint, corrected it in order to harmonize it with the Hebrew text."[9] There is very little hint of this in the NT,[10] nor is there any comparing of the Hebrew version with the LXX, or for that matter of the LXX with other Greek OT translations, but rather clearly Heb 11.23 and 1 Cor 15.54 are closer to Theodotion's Greek text than to the LXX. And this becomes even more of an issue when we are dealing with the church of the second, third, and fourth centuries and the sources its writers used. Already in 1 Clem. 34.6, it appears the author is following a version of Daniel that we find in Theodotion's Greek text.[11]

To understand what exactly is at issue here, Lamarche stresses,

> The Septuagint as a whole is a rereading of the Hebrew Bible, and it is in this Greek form that the primitive Church received the "Old Testament," beginning with the New Testament writers themselves. It should be no surprise, then, that patristic authors read and commented on the Septuagint, that they argued from it, that they supported themselves with it—including its alleged "mistranslations." And they did so without the least naiveté. On the contrary, they were conscious that revelation as a whole had followed a progression and that it had come to the Church in this renewed Greek form. . . . [W]hen faced with the dilemma of "choosing" between the Hebrew Bible and the Septuagint as the "original"

> Bible of the Church, the choice has already been dic-
> tated by the New Testament writers themselves: it is the
> Septuagint.[12]

This is saying too much, but it is basically correct. A scholar like Jerome makes clear that some early Christians realized they needed to reckon with the original Hebrew version of the Old Testament. And this realization became only more widespread the closer we get to the various Reformations.[13]

Already some of the NT writers (e.g., Paul) do indeed show evidence of knowing the Hebrew text and following it in places, but by the time the church had become dominantly gentile, by the time we get to the Greek-speaking church fathers of the post-apostolic era, Lamarche's conclusion is basically right. They relied on the LXX or some Greek OT as their OT Bible. The Greek OT became a primary basis that the church used as sacred writings to lead people to Christ. But this whole evangelistic thrust, using sacred texts on behalf of a variant of Jewish monotheism, when Judaism was not by and large an evangelistic religion, came as a shock to many in the Greco-Roman world.

Alarm bells went off for many people living in the Greco-Roman world that there was a growing number of people in the NT era who subscribed not only to some form of monotheism but also to some sort of collection of inspired texts—holy writings—and were aggressive in sharing these documents and their truths with outsiders, and were *not* simply ordinary diaspora Jews.[14] This was surprising not only because Greco-Roman religions didn't really have the equivalent of a Bible, but also because these cultures were oral cultures. There were many reasons orality was primary in that world, not least of which was that literacy was not at a high level in the culture in general—perhaps 15–20 percent at the utmost, and that chiefly involved the social elites who had had formal education, and overwhelmingly it was elite men who got that education. Written texts in that environment were largely oral texts—meant to be read out loud so all could hear and learn what was said.[15] And so the texts were often shaped so the hearer might be persuaded about something, which is to say they were shaped according to the ancient conventions of rhetoric.[16]

As I have already intimated, into this sort of oral environment came another novelty of history—an evangelistic religion, and not just any sort of religion but a religion that affirmed that all human beings were lost and needed to be saved, and that the message about this salvation needed to be spread far and wide throughout the empire and beyond.[17] And oh by the way, the Greco-Roman gods were not real gods, nor was the emperor! While Plutarch apparently had bemoaned the fact that "nowadays Mt. Olympus is overcrowded," in the Greco-Roman polytheistic world, there was always room for one more deity, unless, of course, it was being suggested there was only one true God—the biblical one.[18]

It is difficult to convey just how novel these Christian ideas were. Religion in antiquity was tied to specific ethnic groups, specific cultures, and specific locations. The essence of those religions involved priests, temples, and literal sacrifices of animals of various sorts. But this new religion had no temples, priests, and sacrifices, nor did it believe that geography, gender, and generation determined people's identities from birth. It believed, rather, in the radical notion that people could really change, that by hearing the message of salvation people could be "converted."

Just how radical this notion of change and conversion was can be seen by reading A. D. Nock's classic study of the ancient Greco-Roman world entitled *Conversion*.[19] Nock theorized that Christianity succeeded where other religions failed by adopting and adapting some of the most appealing features of these other religions. What Nock didn't take into account is factors that can't be readily explained by socialization processes, in particular dramatic and even sometimes sudden changes in personal orientation, direction, belief, and life commitments.

Conversion to becoming a Christ follower often involved more than what sociological analysis can account for, and interestingly even pagan writers knew this and ridiculed the notion of conversion. No one who has read Apuleius' parody of conversion in *The Golden Ass* can doubt that he understood that something mysterious was being claimed about people being able to dramatically change through divine influence.[20] The Latin novel recounts the story of a man who, through his fascination with sex and magic, is turned into an ass and has to have the assistance of the Egyptian goddess Isis to be changed back into a human being. It is clear enough that Apuleius thinks such dramatic changes in a person are asinine, but he knows of people who have claimed to have them in life, including dramatic religious changes.

While there were indeed social factors leading to conversions to Christianity, as Rodney Stark points out,[21] this movement was led by the more socially elite members of the sect, those who were literate and could produce documents with the help of scribes, and the movement was spread in part by the production of many documents, of which twenty-seven later were culled from the many to form a New Testament, a companion to and further development of the OT Scriptures.[22] This was not entirely surprising in the first century when the majority of Christians, and in particular the majority of Christian leaders, were Jews who had been raised on sacred writings and believed in the importance of such documents. But what would motivate more socially elite persons to spearhead such a movement, often at the cost of pressure, persecution, and sometimes even execution? It was not to their social advantage, nor would it help them climb up the *cursus honorum* if they were Romans or had become Roman citizens like Paul the apostle.

So then there were several crucial things that stood out about this offshoot of early Judaism. It shared with Judaism monotheism and the belief that God revealed himself and his will in holy writings that themselves were God-breathed and so true. Paul in one of his first letters puts it this way: "And we also thank God continually because, when you received the word of God, which you heard from us, *you accepted it not as a human word, but as it actually is, the word of God*, which is indeed at work in you who believe" (1 Thess 2.13). He is, of course, talking about the oral proclamation, but as I have shown in my earlier study *The Living Word of God*, Paul believed that the written-down form of such preaching was Scripture, was a holy writing that needed to be embraced and believed.

And clearly, Paul was not alone in such beliefs, for near the end of the first century we hear this in 2 Pet 3.15–16: "Bear in mind that our Lord's patience means salvation, just as our dear brother Paul also wrote you with the wisdom that God gave him. He writes the same way in all his letters, speaking in them of these matters. His letters contain some things that are hard to understand, which ignorant and unstable people distort, *as they do the other Scriptures*, to their own destruction." Paul's letters are categorized as "like the other Scriptures." And this conviction was to carry on throughout the succeeding centuries until the twenty-seven books of the NT canon were recognized in three different regions of the empire as the "new testament," as Christian Holy Writ.

Sometimes this process of delineating what counted as early Christians' own sacred texts is said to have been caused by heresy, for instance, by Marcion (85–160 A.D.) and his truncated canon that excluded OT books, the Gospel of Luke, and some Pauline letters. But as Harry Gamble has stressed, the Gospels and a collection of Paul's letters had already begun to acquire the status of Scripture well before Marcion wrote his list of early Christian books that could be relied on as Scripture.[23] The most one can say is figures like Marcion and the gnostics only furthered the process of forming a NT canon at a more accelerated rate. That process had already been in progress before Marcion said anything in the second century A.D.

THE APOSTOLIC FATHERS AND THE SECOND CENTURY

You can see this process working itself out in the early second century in the writing of an early Christian martyr—Polycarp. Polycarp is an important bridge figure between the apostolic era and the so-called Apostolic Fathers. He lived from about 69 A.D. to the time when he was martyred, perhaps as early as 155. Apart from one trip to Rome, he seems to have spent his entire life in Smyrna, and he became a church leader there, perhaps even a bishop. His name (meaning "much fruit") probably suggests he was a gentile. Sadly, we have only one document penned by him: his letter to the Philippians. But this document is of enormous importance because of the way it treats earlier Christian documents as having scriptural, and so final, authority. It is also important because it demonstrates clearly how many NT documents were already in wide circulation in early Christianity and serving as authoritative sources for doing theology and ethics. Here is a list helpfully compiled by Luke Wilson of Polycarp's source material either by way of citation or allusion:[24]

Matthew (~10x)	1 Thessalonians (~2x)
Mark (1x)	2 Thessalonians (1x)
Luke (~4x)	1 Timothy (~4x)
Acts (~3x)	2 Timothy (~3x)
Romans (~3x)	Hebrews (~2x)
1 Corinthians (~5x)	1 Peter (~14x)
2 Corinthians (~3x)	1 John (~2x)
Galatians (~4x)	3 John (1x)
Ephesians (~4x)	Jude (1x)
Philippians (~5x)	

Notice Polycarp uses all the canonical Gospels except John, which is passing strange if (1) Polycarp met and learned from John son of Zebedee and if (2) the Gospel with the name John was produced by John son of Zebedee. Both notions can and should be doubted. The John Polycarp likely met was one still alive in the 80s and 90s, namely John the elder, who is perhaps also John of Patmos. It is Irenaeus, who was apparently converted by Polycarp, who claims the latter sat at the feet of John son of Zebedee. What we know is that Polycarp knew Papias (who seems to have been the bishop in Laodicea and Hierapolis), and Papias himself says he had only met the elder John, not John the apostle. The same likely applies to Polycarp, not least because now we have papyrus evidence that John son of Zebedee was martyred like his brother early on.[25]

What is striking about the list above is not just that the Gospel of John is not mentioned, but that we have a heavy dependence on Matthew; the Pauline corpus, including the Pastorals, and especially 1 Peter; and significant references to Luke-Acts as well. *An amazing twenty of twenty-seven NT books are quoted or alluded to*, as Polycarp's letter to the Philippians is basically a pastiche of citations and allusions from earlier Christian documents. For our purposes, what is especially important about this is that he treats the material as Scripture, not merely as good Christian tradition.

Christians of the second century were quite prepared to use non-apostolic, non-eyewitness Christian documents, but already there was a distinction between Scripture and tradition when both categories referred to Christian documents. Distinctions were clearly being made in that century between the primary authority, namely Scripture, both OT and early Christian, and other traditions worth reading but that should not be read in Christian meetings or proclaimed. There is the celebrated case of Bishop Serapion of Antioch (191–211 A.D.), who heard about the reading of the Gospel of Peter in some Christian meeting and decided to look into the matter. He read the document itself and declared it was not by Peter and should not be treated as Scripture or read out in church. He presented a clear argument to the church in Rhossus in Syria condemning it and wrote letters to other congregations to the same effect.[26]

And then there is the Acts of Paul and Thecla, which when Tertullian read it at the end of the second century and discovered an elder from the province of Asia had written it, Tertullian had the man defrocked once he confessed to being its author (see *Bapt.* 17.5—190 A.D.). Clearly, genuine apostolic documents and other documents pretending to be by apostolic figures were being made, but there was also a distinction between valuable Christian traditions of the second century and Christian Scriptures as well, though the process took considerable time to sort things out.

Elsewhere, I have written at length about the Muratorian Canon list and its likely second-century origins, not least because it seems to have been compiled by the brother of a church official we know lived in the mid-second century. It attests to the process of compiling and weeding out, and it includes only two documents from the second century, the Shepherd of Hermas and the Apocalypse of Peter, and otherwise only documents from the apostolic era. I would date this list to about 170 or a little earlier.[27]

Here is the crucial passage: "But Hermas wrote *The Shepherd* 'most recently in our time,' in the city of Rome, while bishop Pius, his brother, was occupying the chair of the church of the city of Rome. And therefore, it ought indeed to be read; but it cannot be read publicly to the people in church either among the Prophets, whose number is complete, or among the Apostles, for it is after their time" (author's translation). As for the Apocalypse of Peter, it was popular in the second century, especially in the province of Asia and other adjoining provinces when premillennialism was the dominant form of eschatology, clearly affirmed by Papias and apparently by Polycarp as well. The author of the list, however, feels compelled to mention that "some of us will not allow the Apocalypse of Peter to be read in church."[28] Notice the clear distinction in the list between what should be read in church as a clearly apostolic document and what should not be read in church. Here again the distinction is made between the formative idea of Christian Scriptures that are early, apostolic, and treated like OT Scriptures and other Christian documents that are valuable but not scriptural because not apostolic. Notice as well that the author of the list clearly thinks the Epistles to the Laodiceans and to the Alexandrians are spurious, not by Paul, and not approved Christian reading material in or outside the church. The author ascribes them to Marcion or his supporters to further the heresy of Marcion. This reference further supports the notion that the list was originally compiled in the second century A.D., not later.[29]

Another important figure in the discussion of the second-century gestation period when it comes to what counted as Scripture and what counted as tradition—and what counted as forgeries—is, of course, Tertullian (155–220 A.D.), perhaps the first truly great theologian of the church after the apostolic era and certainly the first great one from Africa (born and died in Carthage). Like his predecessors John of Patmos, Papias, and probably Polycarp, Tertullian affirmed premillenialism. This may in part explain his eventual embrace of Montanism. As for his views on Scripture, we can do no better than to cite the summary available to us from Wikipedia:

> Tertullian did not have a specific listing of the canon; however, he quotes 1 John, 1 Peter, Jude, Revelation, the Pauline Epistles and the four Gospels. After Tertullian's conversion to Montanism, he also started to use the Shepherd of Hermas. Tertullian . . . in his book *Adversus Marcionem* . . . quotes the book of Judith. He quoted most of the Old Testament including many deuterocanonical books, however he never used the books of Chronicles, Ruth, Esther, 2 Maccabees, 2 John, and 3 John. He defended the book of Enoch and he believed that the book was omitted by the Jews from the canon. He believed that the epistle to the Hebrews was [composed] by Barnabas.[30] For Tertullian scripture was authoritative, he used scripture as the primary source in almost every chapter of his every work, and very rarely anything else. He seems to prioritize the authority of scripture above anything else.
>
> When interpreting Scripture, Tertullian would occasionally believe passages to be allegorical or symbolic, while in other places he would support a literal

interpretation. Tertullian would especially use allegorical interpretations when dealing with Christological prophecies of the Old Testament. Tertullian's view of interpretation also included the belief of the simplicity of scripture, he believed that scripture interprets itself, for Tertullian scripture must be interpreted in the light of a greater number of texts and that they need to agree with each other.[31]

On closer inspection, what seems clear is that once Tertullian became a Montanist, some of his views about extracanonical books like the Shepherd of Hermas seem to have changed. Nevertheless, Tertullian quite clearly bears witness to the process of sifting and discernment that distinguished among Scripture, valuable non-scriptural (and orthodox) traditions, and documents and traditions that did not comport with the first two categories and deserved to be avoided, whether they were forgeries or simply contained heterodox teachings and praxis.

The next figure of great importance, which leads us up to the period of canonization, is Irenaeus (130–200 A.D.), probably a convert of Polycarp. He, of course, is famous for being the great opponent of Gnosticism, but there is much more to the man, and our focus needs to be on his view of Scripture and tradition. Here we are helped by an article by Jeffrey Bingham.[32]

Bingham sums up his basic perspective as follows:

> This study argues that for Irenaeus "scripture" includes, first and foundationally, the writings of the prophets and the apostles but also, secondarily and derivatively, the aforementioned writings of Clement, Papias, Polycarp,

and perhaps Hermas. For Irenaeus, then, "scripture" was a broad term, but he maintained a clear bias toward the prophets and apostles as foundational and essential. It is this bias that he passes on and that gives rise to future fourth-century principles of canon building. In this light, scholarly conceptions of the "rise" and "fall" of writings to and from sacred stature become unnecessary.

Following Matthew Steenberg, he adds, "In other words, for Irenaeus 'to refer simply to "the writings" (αἱ γραφαί) or "the writing" (ἡ γραφή), without further qualification, is always and without exception to indicate a passage or concept drawn from a book of scriptural [or biblical] authority which Irenaeus regards as genuine to the Christian tradition according to the teaching of the apostles.'" He continues,

> In the primary place, I argue, "scripture" designated the Old Testament (law and prophets) and the New Testament (evangelists, apostles, and dominical sayings; or simply the prophets and apostles). To help make sense of Irenaeus's taxonomy, I will label this category foundational, ancestral, or primary scripture. Second, Irenaeus uses the term "scripture" to designate certain early Christian documents (like *Hermas* or *1 Clement*) written by those closely associated with the apostles to transmit their teaching. I label this category secondary or derived scripture, using "derived" in the positive sense of drawing upon the foundational teachings of the prophets and apostles. Within this taxonomy, the prophets and apostles are the fountain, and certain writings authored by those closely associated with the apostles are the stream. I argue that Irenaeus labels both categories of texts as scripture but never intends that secondary scriptures be

confused with primary scriptures. Secondary scriptures
are distinct from those scriptures in which the apostles
transmitted the gospel, "the foundation and pillar of our
faith." In using this language, Irenaeus echoes Eph. 2:20,
where Paul identifies the apostles and prophets as the
Church's unique foundation. Thus, Irenaeus has different senses of scripture.[33]

This is very different from the conclusions of N. Geisler in his article "Irenaeus on Scripture and Tradition." He
argues, "Irenaeus declares that 'the Scriptures are indeed
perfect, since they were spoken by the Word of God and
His Spirit' (AH 2.28.2). They are also said to be 'divine'
(from God) and God cannot err (Rom. 3:4; Titus 1:2; Heb.
6:18). They are called 'the Scripture of truth' as opposed to
the 'spurious writings' of heretics (1.20.1). The fact that 'all
Scripture . . . has been given to us by God' is further evidence
of their inerrancy, since God cannot err (AH 2.28.3)."[34]

The problem with this is that Geisler does not take into
account the kind of evidence Bingham presents, but on the
other hand Bingham assumes that wherever the term γραφή
appears, it must mean scripture in some sense. But the term
itself just means "writings." Geisler is correct that Irenaeus
has a very high view of Scripture as being totally truth telling, but he does not reason like Geisler, who has certain
presuppositions like "God cannot err; God spoke the Scriptures; therefore the Scriptures are inerrant." Rather, Irenaeus seems to argue the Scriptures tell the truth about the
things they assert and therefore are clearly divine and from
God. Irenaeus' view includes both the OT, in its Greek translation, and the NT as being preserved by the providence of

God without forgery and a complete account of the truth, admitting no addition or subtraction (*Haer.* 4.33.8).

Irenaeus is even prepared to say that the LXX was "translated under divine inspiration."[35] Outside the NT, Irenaeus valued apostolic tradition, but the preaching of the church must be on the basis of the Scriptures themselves, and even if this preaching draws on such extracanonical traditions, it must be "conformed to Scripture in organic fidelity to the apostles, in a web not woven by human hands but by 'the one steadfast and truthful Teacher, the Word of God.'"[36]

The problem with Bingham is that while I don't doubt Irenaeus affirmed that Papias' writings, 1 Clement, the epistle of Polycarp, and less likely the Shepherd of Hermas were sacred writings in some sense (and certainly not heretical) and therefore valuable for Christian instruction, he does not talk about them as divinely inspired in the same way he talks about OT and apostolic documents. At most he seems to see such valuable documents as deuterocanonical on a par with some of the documents in the LXX. But perhaps that is what Bingham means by secondary scriptures.

Furthermore, as D. Minns points out, Irenaeus does indeed distinguish between the authority of the NT books in the lives of Christians and apostolic tradition. "Although Irenaeus relies so heavily on the writings of both testaments in defining himself as a Christian, he does not regard the scriptures as a *sine qua non* of Christian self-definition. There have been, and are, Christians who are not able to read or write . . . yet hold fully to the true faith handed down from the apostles. What they hold is not in any way different from what is contained in the scriptures, but they have received it, by tradition, without the need for writing (*Haer.* 3.4.2)."[37] Clearly, Irenaeus had a category called *paradosis*, or "tradition," which he distinguished from the Scriptures themselves, and I doubt he simply assumed that the term *graphe* always meant "scripture."

Whatever may be the case, the church fathers in the fourth century did indeed narrow the list of what could be called NT Scripture, the rest being valuable traditions. *What we do not see in any of these discussions is the notion that secondary "writings" have the same or even greater authority than the Scriptures properly so called, both the OT and NT Scriptures. Sacred traditions are invaluable, but they are not viewed as infallible or inerrant, and they are not the final norm for what counts as orthodox. Irenaeus at least does enunciate the idea of a Scripture that is totally true and totally divinely inspired.* Geisler is correct about that.

Origen of Alexandria (185–254 A.D.) deserves mention at this point as well. Lest we think that Irenaeus, because of his allergic reaction to all things gnostic, took a rigid and singular approach to the Scriptures, an examination of Origen's views makes it clear that this is not so. Irenaeus' high view of Scripture is shared by numerous other early church fathers, such as Origen. As Ronald Heine makes quite clear,

> Origen had a very high view of the Bible. He considered Scripture to be divine and inspired. . . . In his many sermons and commentaries Origen makes it clear that he considered the Holy Spirit to be the author of the Biblical books. . . . Even such minor details as Abraham's

> position [under a tree] and Rebecca's daily duties have
> been placed in the Scriptures by the Holy Spirit. We
> will not understand the way Origen reads the Bible if
> we miss this basic point, that it is always the Holy Spirit
> who speaks in the text of the Bible.[38]

This did not mean that Origen thought everything in the
Bible is historically accurate. For example, when he is
talking about the differences between the four Gospels, he
assumes the Gospel writers sometimes made "minor changes
in what happened so far as history is concerned" in order
to convey the spiritual truth. It was the intention of the
evangelists "to speak the truth spiritually and historically at
the same time where that was possible," but where the spiritual truth could be shared only at the expense of detailed
historical accuracy, they chose the spiritual truth (*Comm.
Jo.* 10.19–20). Plenary inspiration doesn't guarantee accuracy
in all the historical details; it guarantees that the spiritual
truth is spoken throughout the Bible. Origen believed that
Scripture was the best interpreter of Scripture, and for him
the hermeneutical key was found in a text like 1 Cor 2.13,
where he places emphasis on the phrase "words taught by
the Spirit, comparing spiritual things with spiritual." This
sentence was taken to mean that the spiritual truth was par-
amount, even if it involved historical distortions at points
(cf. *Selecta in Psalmos*, PG 12:108C).[39]

It is not necessary to retread the territory we already
covered in the discussion of canonization in *The Living Word
of God*;[40] what we do need to examine is some representative

samples of what the patristic fathers said about the authority of Scripture and tradition, to which we now turn.

BEYOND THE SECOND CENTURY

There is perhaps no church father born just before the decisions to make clear what twenty-seven books counted as the New Testament and who did ministry immediately in the wake of that decision that better epitomizes the high view of Scripture and especially great reverence for the Pauline Epistles than John Chrysostom (born in 347 A.D.). Let's start by serving up some of his more telling remarks on Scripture.

1. I exhort and entreat you all, disregard what this man and that man thinks about these things, and inquire from the Scriptures all these things. (*Hom. 2 Cor.* 13.4).

2. The Scriptures . . . bring us to God, and open to us the knowledge of God. (*Hom. Jo.* 59.2)

3. Do you see how it is possible to find in Scripture a remedy appropriate to every trouble afflicting the human race and go off healed? (*Hom. Gen.* 29.4)

4. I do not hear any one glory that he knows the contents, but that he hath a book written in letters of gold. And what gain, tell me, is this? The Scriptures were not given us for this only, that we might have them in books, but that we might engrave them on our hearts. (*Hom. Jo.* 32)

5. From this it is that countless evils have arisen—from ignorance of the Scriptures; from this it is that the plague of heresies has broken out. . . . For as men deprived of this daylight would not walk aright, so they that look not to the gleaming of the Holy Scriptures must needs be frequently and constantly sinning,

in that they are walking in the worst darkness. (*Hom. Rom.*, Argument)

6. Yet if a harper, or dancer, or stage-player call the city, [the citizens] all run eagerly, and feel obliged to him for the call, and spend the half of an entire day in attending to him alone; but when God speaketh to us by Prophets and Apostles, we yawn, we scratch ourselves, we are drowsy. (*Hom. Jo.* 58)[41]

While these quotations provide us with a general picture of Chrysostom's high view of Scripture, a more detailed look at some particulars is necessary and helpful. For example, as Margaret Mitchell has pointed out, in Chrysostom's discussion of 1 Thess 4.13–17, Chrysostom asks why Paul simply speaks the Word of God without in fact quoting God, using a formula like "thus says the Lord," unlike the OT prophets.

> The disparity lies in the different mechanics of divine inspiration: whereas the prophets saw God external to themselves, sitting aloft, for instance, as in the case of Isaiah 6, Paul "had Christ speaking in himself" (2 Cor 13:3; cf. 7:40), so the prophetic mediation thus effected was so immediate as not to require an introductory attribution. Since he was Christ's mouthpiece, Paul did not have to preface his statements to accent their divine authorship, "for the apostle utters the statements of the one who sent him." Paul's prophetic knowledge extended even to the encyclopedic command of exegetical detail he displayed in his writings, which he possessed by the power of the spirit.[42]

Interestingly, Chrysostom doesn't think this exalted view of inspiration in the case of Paul means that Paul had no choice about his calling or what he was going to say. "God does not compel, but allows people to be masters of their own choices even after the call" (*Laud. Paul.* 4.4 [SC 300.188], from Mitchell, *Heavenly Trumpet*, 213). Chrysostom is not reflecting the later theology of Augustine manifested in earlier church history. While affirming the inspiration of the whole Bible, Chrysostom does have a sense of progressive revelation, as the quote above makes clear, which in turn is why he places more emphasis on what he finds in the Pauline Epistles than what he finds in the OT, for example. He doesn't follow the lead of someone like Origen in allegorical or spiritual interpretation, which somehow takes precedent over literal contextual interpretation. For Chrysostom, the historical meaning of the text includes its spiritual substance, and there is no need to prioritize the spiritual over the historical or to compromise the latter for the sake of the former. Origen seems to be the odd man out compared to the other church fathers we have been examining on this sort of issue.[43] This becomes even more the case when one considers someone like Theodoret of Cyrus, who wrote in the fifth century A.D.

Theodoret was adamant that the Scripture in its entirety was fully inspired. And for Theodoret at least, this had some fundamental implications, which Jean-Noël Guinot explains at some length: "From this unity of inspiration arises, in Theodoret's view, the perfect harmony of all Scripture, its *symphônia*. Consequently there are no contradictions within any given book or among diverse scriptural texts, notably among the various prophecies, and there is no disharmony between the Old and New Testaments. 'The divine prophets and holy apostles were all deemed worthy of the same Spirit; thus, they do not contradict one another in what they say, for the Holy Spirit is a spirit of truth.'"[44]

All of the above discussion is more than sufficient to establish that by the time the canon of the NT was clearly defined as involving twenty-seven books, there had already been a very high view of the inspiration and authority of the documents written by the NT writers, an inspiration and authority on par with, if not excelling in some ways, that of the OT despite the complexities of dealing with issues of interpretation.

We have seen clearly that distinctions were made between the Scriptures and other valuable early Christian literature. The former would be the basis of preaching (including evangelism) and teaching; the latter would be used to amplify or clarify what the Scripture said or meant. There was no debate as to whether the OT and NT would be the final court of appeal in all matters of faith and praxis. Nothing else had the same authority, the same inspiration, as those canonical books. But what we do not really find is the idea of *sola Scriptura*, as if other Christian traditions *had no authority at all*. In short, *we find* prima Scriptura *in these early documents, but not a clear articulation of* sola Scriptura, *such that other traditions had no authority or weight at all in settling disputes over important matters. As it happens, we don't really find the concept of* sola Scriptura *clearly and persuasively articulated and argued for another eight hundred years of church history. So we must turn to the fourteenth century.*

2

The Origins of *Sola Scriptura*

> As for the Scriptures, Marsiglius declares them to be
> the ultimate source of authority. They do not derive
> that authority from the Church. The Church gets its
> authority from them.
>
> Schaff, *History of the Christian Church*, 6:76[1]

The story of the ecumenical councils does not need to be rehearsed in this volume, but several points are of relevance. First, neither the Council of Nicaea in 325 A.D. nor the Council of Chalcedon in 450 A.D. nor any of the other early councils was *primarily* about defining or refining Scripture, or clearly stating Scripture's authority in the church. No, they were clearly focused on theological matters, and especially about sorting Christology out. There was not even an ecumenical council on the Holy Spirit (which in part explains the later split between the Western and Eastern church) or, for that matter, on such a crucial matter as the atoning death of Christ.

Having said this, it is true that the Council of Nicaea did recognize and delineate the books of the NT so that Constantine would know which ones should be included in his published anthology of the Christian Scriptures. This was a matter handled with relative dispatch—no major controversy—and therefore is evidence that by 325 catholic Christianity had already in practice determined which texts had scriptural authority. The affirmations about forty or so years later simply officially clarified this matter in regard to which books were included.

After the Council of Nicaea, in 331 Constantine commissioned fifty Bibles to be composed with Eusebius (265–339 A.D.) preparing them, to be used in the growing number of churches in Constantinople. We know about this because Eusebius mentions it in a letter he says came to him from Constantine himself: "I have thought it expedient to instruct your Prudence to order fifty copies of the sacred Scriptures, the provision and use of which you know to be most needful for the instruction of the Church, to be written on prepared parchment in a legible manner, and in a convenient, portable form, by professional transcribers thoroughly practiced in their art." Eusebius reflecting on this says, "Such were the Emperor's commands, which were followed by the immediate execution of the work itself, which we sent him in magnificent and elaborately bound volumes of a threefold and fourfold form" (*Vit. Const.* 4.36–37). This latter sentence probably means in three or four columns per page. It is possible, but uncertain, that this includes what were later called Codex Vaticanus and Codex Sinaiticus. In any case, what we are talking about is a Greek OT plus the twenty-seven NT books plus the Epistle of Barnabas and the Shepherd of Hermas, at least in Sinaiticus. Vaticanus as we have it is not complete.[2]

Overall, the result of these sorts of actions, since there was not an *official* declaration by an ecumenical council about the limits of the canon or a statement about the relationship of the authority of the Bible to the authority of the church and its leaders, is that the authority of church officials, the pope in the West, and patriarchs elsewhere grew and grew and led to some quite unbiblical ideas and pronouncements. The old adage "all power corrupts, and ultimate power corrupts ultimately" turns out to be as true of church leaders as of secular rulers. So, the long history of abuse of power by the hierarchy prompted a clear reaction from various monks, scholars, and laypersons. By the fourteenth century some were prepared to say, at great cost to themselves (and in the case of John Wycliffe, probably his life), ENOUGH IS ENOUGH.[3] The fallback position for all these sorts of persons was the final authority of Scripture; indeed, they were even prepared to talk publicly about the idea of *sola Scriptura*, that the Bible alone has final authority over all matters of faith and praxis.

HISTORICAL PRECURSORS TO THE REFORMATION

It is correct to say that in the fourteenth century, after many abuses of papal authority, in matters political, theological, and ethical, and indeed after two sets of popes, one in Rome and one in Avignon, many Catholics were unhappy with the notion that the final authority, indeed the infallible authority in regard to doctrine and praxis, lay in the hands of the pope.[4] Already in the first decade of the fourteenth century we have the anti-papal tract writers critiquing the traditional notion of the absolute supremacy of the pope's judgment in all matters sacred or secular that affected the church. Interestingly, these writers not only appealed to the ultimate authority of Scripture but to reason, and even to Aristotle and his concern for logic that was in accord with the known facts. These arguments were made because of the tug-of-war between the Papacy and rulers of various regions as to where the final authority lay. Interestingly, Dante, of *Divine Comedy* fame, weighed in on this dispute, arguing like numerous others that the NT insists on respecting the governing authorities and paying one's taxes, and that nothing in the NT suggests that church leaders should have secular authority, even over emperors and kings. In short there was nothing holy about the idea of the Holy Roman Empire.

In 1329, Dante's tract *On the Monarchy* was burned as heretical by order of Pope John XXII. One of the things being dealt with was the infamous forgery the Donation of Constantine, which asserts that Constantine turned over the authority in Rome and the western part of the church (and much more widely as well) to the pope in Rome. In this period, the tractarians were not yet arguing the Donation document was a forgery; they were arguing Constantine shouldn't have done that.

Actually, the debate about the Donation of Constantine had already begun at the turn of the first millennium (in about 1001). The evidence as we have it now suggests that the document was forged in the eighth century A.D. to prop up the authority claims of the Papacy, even over some of the eastern part of the church (Constantinople and Jerusalem). As such it seems to have been part of the ongoing power struggle between the Eastern Greek-speaking churches and the Latin-speaking churches in the West. In 1300 popes began to use the document itself to bolster their authority.

Alas, the document, which purports to have been written by Constantine in March 315 A.D., has obvious errors that Constantine would never have made. It can't even get the date of Constantine's fourth consulate correct! Lest we think that Constantine was allegedly just bequeathing Rome and the Lateran Palace (which are mentioned) to the pope, there is also this sentence that grants to the seat of Peter "power, the dignity of glory, and the vigor and distinction of empire," and "primacy over the four distinguished sees of Antioch, Alexandria, Constantinople, and Jerusalem as well as over all churches of God in the whole globe of earth." For the upkeep of the church of Saint Peter and that of Saint Paul, Constantine is said to have given landed estates "in Judaea, Greece, Asia, Thrace, Africa, and Italy as well as various islands." Among other things, this was an attempt to delegitimize the authority claims of various bishops in the Eastern church, especially those in Constantinople and Jerusalem. You can see this at work in the letter Pope Leo IX sent to the patriarch in Constantinople in 1054, in which Leo quotes the Donation text at length to make his claim of authority over Patriarch Michael I Cerularius.

In 1439–1440 Lorenzo Valla, an Italian priest and one of the great linguistic scholars of his day, whom we will have occasion in the next chapter to speak more about, was the first to do a full and proper exposé of the forged nature of the Donation of Constantine, through his usual detailed philological analysis of the document. But even before him there were brave souls in the Catholic Church who in good conscience had to object to what was going on.

One such person embroiled in this whole struggle between spiritual and secular authorities was an Italian scholar named Marsilius of Padua (1270–1342). Trained in medicine and philosophy at the University of Paris, Marsilius wrote a political tract entitled *Defensor Pacis*. In it he accused the pope of gross overreach of authority and power in matters of both church and state. He denied that the pope had "a plenitude of power" in such areas. He was to articulate a position later adopted by both Luther and Calvin, but what exactly did he say?

Most of the arguments in this tract were based soundly in Scripture. For example, Marsilius pointed out that Jesus, unlike Pope John XXII, did not claim to possess temporal power; indeed, he said his kingdom was not of this world! And, furthermore, he instructed his followers (as did Paul later) to obey the existing authorities and not try to exercise any nonecclesial powers. Following Aristotle (his philosophical hero), Marsilius advocated for a democratic form of government, with the people themselves having the ultimate authority and rulers being their representatives.

As for authority in the church, the only final authority rests with Scripture, and it appears that Marsilius was the first to interject the phrase *sola Scriptura* into the discussion.[5] He also argued that church councils, not the pope, should be the arbiter and decider in regard to theological and scriptural disputes. The pope is simply one priest among many, and there is no evidence Peter was made the first pope of Rome by Christ. Not surprisingly, Marsilius was declared a heretic by the pope.

Marsilius' *Defensor Pacis* is said by Philip Schaff to be "as audacious as any of the earlier writings of Luther. For originality and boldness of statement the Middle Ages has nothing superior to offer. . . . Its Scriptural radicalism was in itself a literary sensation."[6] Like William of Ockham (on which see below), Marsilius rejected the Donation of Constantine, as Dante had done before him.[7]

Marsilius is perfectly clear that the Scriptures are the ultimate source of authority *and that they do not derive their authority from the church. To the contrary, the church gets its authority from the Scriptures.* Unlike Aquinas, who followed Marsilius by fifty years, Marsilius did not perpetuate the false interpretations of Scripture that had been used to give the Papacy scriptural legitimacy by the Schoolmen. To the contrary, he regularly cited Jesus' pronouncements "my kingdom is not of this world" and "render unto Caesar what is Caesar's and to God what is God's" to support the separation of church and state powers, and the legitimacy of secular power as not beholden or subservient to the church. He also cites John 6.15, 19.11; Luke 12.14; Matt 17.27; and Rom 13 to good purpose.

William of Ockham (1287–1347), an English Franciscan friar, was another figure involved in challenging papal authority, and again on the basis of Scripture. He argues that even popes can be heretical and must be challenged on the basis of Scripture, citing the example of Paul calling Peter to task and confronting him for his "Judaizing" (see Gal 2). The pope, argues William, is not infallible, and indeed the Papacy itself is not necessary to the being or well-being of the church. Furthermore, a church council can also err. William assumes that the Donation of Constantine is a legitimate historical argument and argues that it proves that the pope did *not* originally have secular power, but rather it had to be given to him by Constantine. William is perfectly clear that popes and councils may err, and that the Bible alone is inerrant. A Christian cannot and should not be held to believe anything not in the canon of Scripture itself.[8] Luther was later to call him "my dear teacher."

Another important figure that spoke about such matters before Luther was John Wycliffe of England (1328–1384). Like Marsilius, he was a philosopher and a Catholic priest, but in addition he was a Bible translator, theologian, reformer, and professor at Oxford. Among other things, he questioned the privileged status of clergy and advocated and undertook the translation of the Bible into the vernacular English of his day without official permission. There is some debate as to whether he translated the whole of the NT, and in any case his source text was the Latin Vulgate, not the Greek. His associates did the OT translation. It was already completed by about 1384.

Like Marsilius, Wycliffe questioned the authority of the Papacy and affirmed that the Scriptures, even in translation, should have the final authority in matters of faith and practice. One of the last things that Wycliffe wrote and affirmed before his death in 1384 was that the ultimate authority for the church lay in the Scriptures, and that the claims of the Papacy to such authority were unhistorical. His position on this matter became even clearer and more emphatic the longer he lived. He was even prepared to say that the Scriptures were the only reliable and authoritative guide to the truth about God. His position foreshadowed the later claims of Luther in regard to *sola Scriptura*.

All three of these examples (Marsilius, William of Ockham, Wycliffe), as well as the later ones from the Reformation, suggest that mainly what prompted ideas such as sola Scriptura *were the abuses of power by the pope and the failure of the Papacy to simply follow biblical teaching or its logical implications and applications.* But we must consider Wycliffe more closely. Even his friend Geoffrey Chaucer (1342–1400) seems to have praised him in part of his *Canterbury Tales*, "The Poor Parson." A few of the relevant verses are worth quoting about Wycliffe's character:

> A kindly Parson took the journey too.
> He was a scholar, learned, wise, and true.
> And rich in holiness though poor in gold.
> A gentle priest: whenever he was told
> That poor folks could not meet their tithes that year,
> He paid them up himself; for priests, it's clear
> Could be content with little, in God's way.
> He lived Christ's Gospel truly every day,
> And taught his flock, and preached what Christ had said.
> And even though his parish was widespread . . .
>
> The Shepherd must perfect
> His life in holiness that all his sheep
> May follow him, although the way is steep,
> And win at last to heaven. Indeed, I'm sure
> You could not find a minister more pure.
> He was a Christian both in deed and thought;
> He lived himself the Golden Rule he taught.[9]

John Wycliffe is quite rightly called the "morning star of the Reformation." He was nothing if not bold in his critique of the Papacy, even at one point later in life calling the pope the antichrist of Revelation (and Luther was to follow him in this pronouncement). It is in about 1378 that he really began his crusade of reform. At this point there were two popes in two different cities, and for Wycliffe this was enough to properly shake confidence in the notion that the Papacy itself was of divine or scriptural origin, never mind all the previous abuses and false teaching that had come forth from popes.

Wycliffe was equally bold in taking on the pronounce-ments of the Fourth Lateran Council about the doctrine of transubstantiation. No, said Wycliffe, that is not a scrip-tural idea. Christ is only present figuratively in the Eucha-rist; the bread and wine remain bread and wine. This and other pronouncements were condemned by a council in 1382 convoked by the archbishop of Canterbury. John was forced to retire to Lutterworth, his parish, and from there he con-tinued to work on his translation of the Bible and put forth a notable tract entitled *Trialogus*, in which he insisted that where the Bible and the church don't agree, the Bible must be followed, and where conscience and human authority don't agree, conscience must be followed. He did not agree with the determinism of Augustine and others but insisted that the doctrine of necessity does not do away with the freedom of the will. Necessity may compel the individual to make a choice, but he is still free to choose his response.

As for who could proclaim the truth of Scripture, Wycliffe argued that the pope has no exclusive right to declare what the Scriptures teach. In his interpretation of Matt 16.18, he argues clearly that yes, Peter is the rock Jesus refers to, but that rock stands for every true Christian who makes the confession Peter did.[10] The keys to the kingdom were not given exclusively to Peter but to all the saints.

Further, true contrition of the heart is enough for forgiveness; confession is not absolutely necessary to achieve that end, but it can be good for one's spiritual health.

Wycliffe in fact wrote his tract of one thousand printed pages (possibly the last thing he ever wrote) on the value and authority of the Scriptures, and as Schaff points out, "In his treatise . . . more is said . . . than was said by all the mediaeval theologians together. And none of the Schoolmen, from Anselm and Abaelard to Thomas Aquinas and Duns Scotus, exalted it [Scripture] to such a position of preëminence as did he."[11] Unlike the Schoolmen he did not try to coordinate or reconcile Scripture to preexisting tradition. Instead, he insisted Scripture was the final authority and court of appeal in all such matters of doctrine and discipline, of faith and practice.

All things necessary for salvation are found in the Scriptures and do not require supplementation. The Bible is the whole truth that all Christians should study and should be able to study in their own language. The Scripture is the measure of all logic, not the other way around. God speaks in all the books; they are all one great Word of God. Every syllable of the two testaments is true. The human writers were just scribes taking down God's Word. Nothing is necessary to be believed that is not found in this Book, and nothing needs to be added to it. The literal verbal sense of the text is the true one. Other meanings, such as the allegorical one, must be grounded and based in the literal. In 1229 the Council of Toulouse had forbidden laypersons to study and use the Bible! Wycliffe thought this was heresy; withholding the Bible from the laity was a serious sin indeed.

Wycliffe was the first to give the Bible in the vernacular to his own people. Luther later followed suit in German. But this is hardly all. Schaff summarizes things as follows:

> In looking over the career and opinions of John Wyclif, it becomes evident that in almost every doctrinal particular did this man anticipate the Reformers. The more his utterances are studied, the stronger becomes this conviction. He exalted preaching; he insisted upon the circulation of the Scriptures among the laity; he demanded purity and fidelity of the clergy; he denied infallibility to the papal utterances, and went so far as to declare that the papacy is not essential to the being of the Church. He defined the Church as the congregation of the elect; he showed the unscriptural and unreasonable character of the doctrine of transubstantiation; he pronounced priestly absolution a declarative act. He dissented from the common notion about pilgrimages; he justified marriage on biblical grounds as honorable among all men; he appealed for liberty for the monk to renounce his vow, and to betake himself to some useful work.
>
> The doctrine of justification by faith Wyclif did not state. However, he constantly uses such expressions as . . . to believe in Christ is life. The doctrine of merit is denied, and Christ's mediation is made all-sufficient. He approached close to the Reformers when he pronounced "faith the supreme theology" . . . and that only by the study of the Scriptures is it possible to become a Christian.[12]

As intimated above, one other very noticeable element of Wycliffe's theology was that he is not an Augustinian, unlike Luther, or later Calvin. He does not believe the decision to follow Christ is predetermined by God. Rather, he believes each person has the power of contrary choice, even if that is true because grace has enabled a fallen person to make such a choice. Wycliffe believed God is perfectly capable by his grace and providence to provide the church through his inspiration with a completely true and trustworthy Holy Scripture, *without* resorting to the predetermination of everything and everyone before the foundation of the world.

In this regard he foreshadows neither the German nor the Swiss Reformers but rather his fellow English Reformers, such as John Wesley. We will have much to say about Wesley's affirmation of *sola Scriptura* later in this study, but for now we must turn in earnest in our next chapter to look at the events that led to and involved the doctrine of Scripture in the German Reformation. First, however, some things need to be said about events and precursors in the Renaissance that made the Reformation possible.

LINGUISTIC PRECURSORS TO THE REFORMATION

To understand the Bible and its role in the various Reformations, German, Swiss, and English, it is necessary to go back to the Renaissance and get a running start.[13] The Franciscan Roger Bacon shortly after 1266 pled in the first part of his *Opus majus* for the study of "tongues," including the Semitic languages Hebrew and Aramaic, not only because church life in the West was dominated by a secondary language that the Bible was not originally written in, namely Latin, but also because of (1) the conversion of unbelievers, and (2) fundamental errors and numerous false statements in the key Latin theological texts that were the basis for church teaching.[14] Because Bacon's word carried so much weight, the Council of Vienne, which ended in 1312, insisted that chairs in Hebrew, Aramaic, Arabic, and Greek should be founded at the major European universities in Oxford, Paris, Bologna, Salamanca, and Avignon (then the seat of the Papacy).

The spirit of the Renaissance, the desire to go back *ad fontes* and study ancient texts in their original languages to improve on existing translations and establish the most reliable texts possible, had finally prompted the church divines to do something to take advantage of this trend. Yes, one of the main reasons for this was to convert Jews and Muslims to Christianity, but it is also true that it was recognized that the Bible should be studied in its original languages, and that good theology and ethics should be based on such study. In the Middle Ages, it was rare indeed to find a Christian theologian who emulated Jerome's knowledge of the original biblical languages. One of these few was the Venerable Bede of Jarrow (and Durham), the writer of the *Ecclesiastical History of England*, a work that settled the issue in the Western calendar regarding when *anno Domini* began and when B.C. ended.[15]

The center of the Renaissance was originally Italy, and it was in Florence that Giannozzo Manetti mastered Hebrew from local converts from Judaism in about 1440. Like Bacon and others, he had a concern about the Latin Vulgate and its accuracy. Between 1455 and 1458 he translated the NT from the Greek and the Psalms from the Hebrew.

As interest in Hebrew (and Greek) spread among Christian professors, in 1506 Konrad Pellikan issued what is probably the first Hebrew grammar produced by a Christian. But what about Aramaic? There were Aramaic portions of the OT (Jer 10.11; Ezra 4.8–6.18, 7.12–26; Dan 2.4–7.28). Sante Pagnini was the first Christian to issue an Aramaic dictionary in 1523, but it was Sebastian Münster who first clearly distinguished Aramaic from Hebrew in 1527, publishing an Aramaic grammar.

It is fair to say that actual knowledge of Greek in the Christian West was very rare in the late Middle Ages, though it never died out entirely. Of course, in the Christian East this was not a problem, but the Protestant Reformation did not arise as a response to the various Orthodox traditions; it arose as a response to Roman Catholicism and the Latin Vulgate Bible.[16] Prior to the Reformation, things were actually *working backward*. From the ninth to the thirteenth centuries, Western scholars were busily translating Greek texts into Latin, the language of the Western church! This is actually why Luther learned Greek in the first place, so he could translate Greek texts into the language of the Western church—Latin!

Again, it was the Renaissance, its humanist movement and desire to get back to source texts (whether classical or biblical) in their original languages, and particularly the work of Petrarch that helped spur on this trend. Petrarch's interest was focused on the classics, in particular Homer's *Odyssey* and *Iliad* and some works of Plato, but this interest led him to get Leonzio Pilato of Calabria to give lectures on Greek in Florence from 1360–1362. In the early 1380s Simone Atumano, a Basilian monk, gave private Greek lessons in Rome, where he was working on a planned trilingual edition of the Bible (in Hebrew, Greek, and Latin). One other factor of note is that various humanist scholars sailed to Byzantium/Constantinople to learn Greek there in the early 1400s.

Cristoforo Persona actually became a part of the household in Constantinople of Cardinal Isidore of Kiev, who was a theologian, and he learned Greek there. Of especial importance is Guarino da Verona, who also studied Greek in Constantinople. He came back to Italy and introduced Greek into the curriculum in Italian schools in Venice, Florence, and Verona, eventually setting up his own school in Ferrara in 1429. Students from all over Europe flocked there to learn Greek and Latin, including, importantly, Robert Flemmyng and John Free from England. The school became well-known for its students becoming proficient enough in Greek to translate works of Plutarch, Aesop, and John Chrysostom *into Latin*.

All of this is important because in 1453, Constantinople fell to the Osmanli Turks, the ones we call the Ottomans (thanks to British mispronunciations of the group's name). I need to stress that the main interest in learning Greek during this period was in reading and teaching Greek philosophy and rhetoric. *The Bible was not the main focus of this academic thrust.* Nevertheless, the humanists *were mostly not secularists*; indeed, many of their leading lights were devout Christians. Schools found Christian texts already familiar to Western students in Latin very helpful for beginners learning Greek—for example, they would learn to translate the Lord's Prayer or the beginning of the Ave Maria from Greek.

Battista Guarini was to point out that biblical texts were "admirably adapted" for learning on one's own since "there are some texts . . . where a verse in the Latin translation is not a syllable longer or shorter than the Greek original."[17] Thus, it was thought students would readily pick up the vocabulary and syntax by comparing the two language texts. The main reason given for studying Greek in the fifteenth century was to enhance one's knowledge of Latin, and it was done because the ancient Romans knew the Greek, in particular because the famous rhetorician Quintilian said that Latin literature flowed out of Greek literature and language; for example, Virgil in his *Aeneid* imitated Homer.

Pope Nicholas V (who ruled from 1447 to 1455) was himself a humanist, and he sponsored Greek education and translation of Greek texts into Latin. He commissioned George of Trebizond to translate Eusebius' *Preparatio evangelica* and the works of Gregory of Nazianzus, Gregory of Nyssa, and John Chrysostom. You will notice I have not mentioned any focus on the Greek NT, or indeed any dealing with the Bible at all, in these humanistic projects, except indirectly through the translations of some of the Greek fathers. This is, of course, because the language of the church, its liturgy, and its biblical texts was Latin, and in the case of the Bible the Latin Vulgate, which of course was centuries old, going back ultimately to Jerome. As Jill Kraye says, "The Bible occupied only a marginal position in fifteenth-century Greek studies, the main thrust of which was directed towards classical and, to a smaller extent, patristic texts."[18]

Much can be said about the work of the great linguist Lorenzo Valla, who could even be said to be the father of modern text criticism for his comparison of the Latin Vulgate to at least seven different manuscripts of the Greek NT. Valla was careful, focusing on issues of grammar, vocabulary, and style in his some two thousand annotations; nevertheless, he was able to find a whole range of mistakes in the Vulgate that needed to be brought into line with the original Greek text and, as he was to say, with *the truth* of the original text of the NT.[19] A language-based, rather than a philosophically based, approach to the biblical text was what he said we should give priority to, and he could hardly hide his contempt for medieval exegetes like Thomas Aquinas who "dared" to interpret the NT while being totally ignorant of the Greek.[20] Not surprisingly, Valla never published his "Annotationes" during his lifetime, though they circulated in a few circles, including that of Pope Nicholas.

Very, very few copies of Valla's two major works ("Collatio," "Annotationes") were made, but Erasmus had the good fortune of finding a copy of them both in the Abbey of Parc just outside Leuven in 1504, and they were both printed in Paris on his insistence in 1505. "This momentous event for the history of the Bible shows that sometimes what matters is not how many people read a book, but who reads it."[21] To give but one example of the importance of Valla's work to Erasmus, and to his later Greek NT, Valla insisted that the Vulgate of John 21.22 was corrupt in its reading "sic eum volo manere donec veniam . . . ," which we would translate "so I wish him to remain until I come," but the Greek has "*if* I wish him to remain . . ." In the Latin, this amounted to a small emendation of "sic" to "si," but it also meant going against Jerome, whom many would say knew Greek better than anyone in the fifteenth century. And yet Chrysostom and Origen were clear that Jesus said "if." It was a conditional statement.

The NT was the flash point when it came to the matter of rewriting the Bible, or better said, getting back to what the earliest text said. The proof of this was that in 1481 a bilingual psalter was published with a new Latin translation on the facing page with the LXX Greek text. This produced exactly no reaction or criticism at all. What did produce an enormous reaction was the second edition of Erasmus' Greek New Testament, and, of course, Luther's use of it and his subsequent actions. To the latter we must turn in the next chapter.

3

The German and Swiss Reformation

Scripture as the Final Authority

> Since then your serene majesty and your lordships seek a
> simple answer, I will give it in this manner, neither horned
> nor toothed: Unless I am convinced by the testimony of
> the Scriptures or by clear reason (for I do not trust either
> in the pope or in councils alone, since it is well known
> that they have often erred and contradicted themselves),
> I am bound by the Scriptures I have quoted and my con-
> science is captive to the Word of God. I cannot and I will
> not recant anything, since it is neither safe nor right to go
> against conscience. . . . May God help me. Amen.
>
> Martin Luther, *Reply to the Diet of Worms*, April 18, 1521[1]

"ERASMUS LAID THE EGGS THAT LUTHER HATCHED"[2]

There is much to be said for the suggestion that the objections to revising the Latin Vulgate on the basis of the Greek text in the fifteenth century were to be replayed in modernity by Protestants who decided that the KJV was sacrosanct, the completely inerrant translation of the Bible, and that it shouldn't be revised or tampered with in light of the Masoretic Text of the Old Testament or the Greek New Testament. *Plus ça change, plus c'est la même chose*, at least when it comes to the history of the Bible and its authority.

What one would have expected on the basis of Valla's work, and then later in the work of Giannozzo Manetti, who knew both Hebrew and Greek and worked on rendering the Psalms, was that there would be a revision of the Vulgate. But Pope Nicolas, who had supported this work, died in 1455, and Manetti himself died in 1459, and the moment when change could have happened passed. It would be quite late in the sixteenth century, more than a hundred years later, that such a project would be undertaken in earnest. By then, the Protestant bull had left the barn, Erasmus had produced his Greek NT, Luther his German translation, and Tyndale his English one, and there would be no looking back. I need to stress again that Valla's work survived in very few manuscripts and did not have a major impact, except on Erasmus, whereas Manetti's work was basically unknown until the twentieth century. Erasmus is *the* crucial figure.

"It was Desiderius Erasmus who rescued Valla's scriptural labours from obscurity. Erasmus stumbled across the manuscript of the *Annotationes* at the abbey of Parc, near Leuven, in 1504, and published it the following year."[3] Surprisingly, there was no pushback. Erasmus was prepared for criticism when he prepared his Greek NT, however, and he got it, though there was a bit of a delayed response. The first edition in 1516 produced few ripples, but the second edition, published in 1519, set off the alarm bell. Erasmus would argue that correcting errors in a translation or a copy of an original biblical text did not in any way amount to disputing the inspiration of the divinely inspired text. If someone argued it was impious to change anything in Holy Writ, he retorted that *it must be worse then to allow scribal errors to stand uncorrected, as they obscured the original meaning of Scripture!*

Erasmus, in fact, when he published his own annotations, not only borrowed Valla's title but simply reran various of Valla's notes. Note that Jacques Lefèvre d'Étaples also followed Valla's lead and mentioned him in his 1512 commentary on Paul's Epistles. This is important for our purposes because Lefèvre's is the work on which Martin Luther based his game-changing Wittenburg lectures in 1515–1519. And here is where I note that it was Lefèvre's commentary on Romans that produced the phrase "by faith alone," which seems to have been noticed by no one—*except Luther*, who then mistranslated Rom 1.17 as "for the righteousness of God was revealed by faith alone," which actually reads, δικαιοσύνη γὰρ Θεοῦ ἐν αὐτῷ ἀποκαλύπτεται ἐκ πίστεως εἰς πίστιν.[4] That last phrase can be rendered "from faith for faith" or "from the faithful (one) unto faith," but it cannot be rendered "by faith alone." So much for the Lutheran stress on *sola fide*.

Erasmus' first edition of his Greek NT appeared in 1516 and had a facing Latin translation on each page, with a plethora of textual annotations. The early reactions to the first edition were largely favorable, except for Lefèvre's criticism of the translation of Heb 2.7 ("thou hast made him a little lower than the angels"). He argued that it should have read like the original Hebrew, which had the probable reading "a little lower than God" (depending on what one makes of *elohim* in Ps 8.6). Lefèvre argued that the author of Hebrews surely must have originally followed the Hebrew, but Erasmus was simply following the Vulgate of the OT word for word at this point, which in turn was an exact rendering of the original Greek. It was an objection that insinuated Erasmus was flirting with heresy, since Christ could not be lower than the angels. Erasmus was deeply hurt by this objection, coming as it did from a well-respected scholar. Erasmus wrote a fiery response, an apologia really, and had a difficult time moving on.

As Richard Rex says, it really was the emergence of Luther, and his own critiques of Catholicism, that led to a more profound and widespread critique of Erasmus and the whole humanist enterprise of text criticism in an effort to recover the original texts of ancient manuscripts. For example, Johann Eck, who had already taken public exception to Luther and various of his theses, in February 1518 added to that complaint his own misgivings about the work of Erasmus. There were hostile sermons against Erasmus in Bruges, Cologne, and Leipzig in 1518 and from Antwerp, Louvain, and Strasbourg in 1519.

When one gets to the spring of 1519, a conspiracy theory was being noised about that Luther and Erasmus were in league together. It was true that in that same year Luther wrote Erasmus looking for his support. Erasmus, however, demurred, having no wish to be leading the charge of "a new movement." Luther of course had no such qualms. He would be the standard-bearer for the first major salvo that came to be called the Reformation.

Erasmus noted later that he had heard a sermon in 1521 in Paris identifying the four horsemen of the apocalypse—Luther in Germany, Lefèvre in France, an anonymous Franciscan in Italy, and Erasmus himself in the

Netherlands. And this critique was to go on. Diego López de Zúñiga entered into a ten-year-long pamphlet war with Erasmus, accusing him of heresy and being the source of Lutheranism (in 1522). Erasmus responded in 1524 by pointing out that he disagreed with Luther on the issue of the freedom of the will, which helped him to get the Vatican to tell Zúñiga to call off the barking dogs. On the whole, Rex's judgment seems mostly apt that "the story of the 'humanist Bible controversies,' then, should not be told as a whiggish narrative of philological progress paving the way for theological revolution. It was the Reformation that made biblical humanism controversial."[5] Not quite. There had already been some objections to the text-critical enterprise of Valla and Manetti before Luther entered the fray with his Ninety-Five Theses.

What is the case is that the rise of Luther led to increased criticism of Erasmus, including the odium of theological heresy, as people began to realize the connection between revising translations of the Bible based on the Hebrew and Greek originals, which in turn meant revising some deeply cherished medieval theological and historical notions that proved to be wrong (e.g., the association of Mary Magdalene with Mary of Bethany and the sinner woman of Luke 7). If Holy Writ was to have the last word on theology and ethics and praxis, one needed to know *what the original inspired text actually said.* In our final section of this chapter, we must turn to the production of the Bible itself, in the age of Luther.[6]

SOLA SCRIPTURA—BUT WHICH ONE?
The age of the printed book had begun already in the mid-1450s in Mainz with the so-called Gutenberg Bible. This

was simply the Latin Vulgate, the Bible Jerome had produced in Latin in 380 A.D. It was the Catholic Bible, and so it included both a translation of the Hebrew OT and the Greek NT, plus Tobit, Judith, Wisdom of Solomon, Sirach, Baruch, some additions to the book of Daniel, plus 1 and 2 Maccabees. This was indeed by and large the Bible that existed in the West at the time of Luther and the beginning of the Reformation in 1517.[7] De facto Jerome's Vulgate was still the Bible heard in churches and recited as part of the Catholic liturgy, whatever small revisions were being made by scholars in their own writings and publications.

It needs to be understood that at this point in history, the Bible was not a book owned by the general public. There were pulpit Bibles usually chained to the pulpit, there were manuscripts of Bibles in monasteries, there were Bibles owned by kings and the socially elite, but the Bible was not a book possessed by many. Furthermore, the Bible was basically not in the language of the people. Yes, the well-educated socially elite could read Latin, but your average resident of England or France or Germany or Italy or Spain knew only snippets from the Latin Mass. And indeed, often enough they garbled the snippets they knew. For example, the Latin for Jesus' words "this is my body" is "hoc est corpus meum." Some have theorized that this was transformed by a layperson into "hocus pocus." If you want to get a good feel for how bad the situation was in terms of biblical literacy in the general public in this era, read Chaucer's *Canterbury Tales*, written between 1387 and 1400 in Middle English.

Luther realized that if change were really going to happen, it would not come just by debating theology with other

learned souls in the sixteenth century. The Bible needed to
be made available in the vernacular, in this case in German.
In my view, the most dangerous thing Luther ever did was
not nail his Ninety-Five Theses to a door. It was translating into ordinary German first the NT in 1522 and then the
full Bible by 1534, which included what came to be called
the Apocrypha, those extra books from intertestamental
Judaism. Luther kept revising it right into his waning years
of life, for he realized what a major change agent this act of
translating was.

But what version of, for instance, the Greek NT did
Luther base his translation on? It was none other than
Erasmus' much-critiqued second edition of the Greek NT.
Luther was not afraid of controversy, and he did not hesi-
tate to use Erasmus' work. He did not translate directly from
the Latin Vulgate, and for some this amounted to heresy.
As I mentioned earlier, Luther had learned Greek the usual
way, at Latin school at Magdeburg, so he could translate
Greek works into Latin. There are tales, probably true, that
Luther would make forays into nearby towns and villages
just to listen to people speak so that his translation, particularly of the NT, would be as close to ordinary contemporary German usage as possible. This was not to be a Bible of
and for the elite.

Philip Schaff, the great church historian, opined, "The
richest fruit of Luther's leisure in the Wartburg [castle], *and the
most important and useful work of his whole life, is the translation
of the New Testament,* by which he brought the teaching and
example of Christ and the Apostles to the mind and heart of
the Germans in life-like reproduction. . . . He made the Bible

the people's book in church, school, and house."[8] This act by Luther opened Pandora's box when it came to translations of the Bible, and there was no getting the box closed thereafter. Needless to say, it worried church officials of all stripes because they no longer had strict control of God's Word.

Too few people however have said enough about the *precursors* to Luther's act of translating the Bible into the vernacular. For example, John Wycliffe's team preceded Luther by a good 140 years with his translation of the Bible into Middle English between 1382 and 1395. Wycliffe himself was not solely responsible for the translation; others, such as Nicholas of Hereford, are known to have done some of the translating. The difference between the work of the Wycliffe team and Luther is that no textual criticism was involved, by which I mean the Wycliffe team worked directly from the Latin Vulgate. Not so Luther.

In addition, Wycliffe included not only what came to be called the Apocrypha; he threw in 2 Esdras and the second-century work Epistle to the Laodiceans (purportedly by Paul) as a bonus. Like the work of Luther, Wycliffe's work was not authorized by any ecclesiastical or royal authority, but it became enormously popular. The blowback against this act by Wycliffe was severe. Henry IV and his archbishop Thomas Arundel worked hard to suppress the work, and at the Oxford Convocation of 1408 it was voted that *no new translation of the Bible should be made by anyone without official approval*. Wycliffe, however, had struck a match, and there was no putting out the fire.

Perhaps the most poignant tale of this era is not Luther's, but that of William Tyndale, who lived from 1494–1536 and was martyred for his translating of the Bible into English. Tyndale, like Luther, translated directly from the Hebrew and the Greek, leaving the Latin Vulgate out of the process, except presumably for cross-referencing and checking. He actually only finished about half his OT translation, and all of the NT, but since he lived in the age of the printing press, his was the first mass-produced Bible in English.

Tyndale had acquired a copy of Luther's work, but he too relied on Erasmus as the basis for his translation of the NT. Tyndale originally sought permission from Bishop Cuthbert Tunstall of London to produce this work but was told that it was forbidden, indeed heretical, and so Tyndale went to the Continent to get the job done. A partial edition was printed in 1525 (note the date and compare the date of Luther's publication) in Cologne, but spies betrayed Tyndale to the authorities, and ironically he fled to Worms, the very city where Luther himself was brought before a diet and tried. From *there* Tyndale's complete edition of the NT was published in 1526.[9]

As Alister McGrath was later to note, the so-called King James Bible, or Authorized Version, of the early 1600s (in several editions including the 1611 one) was *not* an original translation of the Bible into English but instead a rather wholesale taking over of Tyndale's translation with some help from the Geneva Bible and other translations.[10] Many of the memorable turns of phrase in the King James that became standard English—"by the skin of his teeth," "am I my brother's keeper?" "the spirit is willing but the flesh is weak," "a law unto themselves"—are in fact phrases that Tyndale coined. He had a remarkable gift for turning biblical phrases into memorable English. Indeed, the KJV owed Tyndale a mighty debt for its memorable English prose.

But even the Authorized Version was not the first authorized English translation of the Bible. That distinction goes to the Great Bible of 1539, authorized by Henry VIII himself. Henry wanted this Bible read in all the Anglican churches, and Miles Coverdale produced the translation. Basically, Coverdale simply cribbed from Tyndale's version, with a few objectionable features removed, and he completed Tyndale's translation of the OT plus the Apocrypha. Note, however, that Coverdale used the Vulgate and Luther's translation in making this translation. In fact, he did *not* use the original Hebrew or Greek, but rather *previous translations*.

For this and various other reasons, many of the budding Protestant movements on the Continent and in Great Britain were not happy with the Great Bible. The Geneva Bible had more vivid and vigorous language and quickly became more popular than the Great Bible. It was the Bible of choice of William Shakespeare, Oliver Cromwell, John Bunyan, John Donne, and the pilgrims when they came to New England. It was the Bible that accompanied them on the *Mayflower, not the KJV*.

One of the things that made this Geneva version of the Bible popular was not only that it was mass-produced for the general public but that it had a variety of annotations, study guides, cross-references to relevant verses elsewhere in the Bible, introductions to each book, summarizing content, maps, tables, illustrations, and even indexes. In short, it was the first study Bible in English, and again note, it preceded the KJV by a half century. Not surprisingly for a Bible produced under the aegis of John Calvin's Geneva, the notes were Calvinistic in substance and Dissenting in character, which is one of the things that prompted the kings of England to respond and produce the Authorized Version. They needed a Bible that didn't question *deus et mon droit*.

AND SO?

Luther could not have imagined in 1517 that his most influential act during the German Reformation, the act that would touch the most lives and effect the budding Protestant movement the most, would not be his Galatians or Romans commentaries, or his theological tracts like *The Bondage of the Will*, or even his insistence on justification by grace through faith alone. No, the biggest rock he threw into the ecclesiastical pond, which produced not only the most ripples but real waves, was the Luther Bible. But he was not alone. He and William Tyndale deserve equal billing as the real pioneers of translating the Bible from the original languages into the language of ordinary people, so they might read it, study it, learn it, and be moved and shaped by it. The Bible of the people, by the people, and especially for the people did not really exist before Luther and Tyndale.

Today, to speak just of English, there are more than nine hundred translations or paraphrases of the NT in whole or in part into our language. Nine hundred! None of the original Reformers could have envisioned this, nor for that matter could they have imagined many people having Bibles not just in the pulpits and pews but in their own homes. The genie that was let out of the bottle at the beginning of the German Reformation turned out to be the Holy Spirit, who makes all things new. This includes ever-new translations of the Bible, as we draw closer and closer to the original inspired text of the Old and New Testaments, through the discovery of more manuscripts, the hard work of text criticism, and translation based on our earliest and best witnesses to the Hebrew, Aramaic, and Greek texts of the Bible.

When the Luther Bible was produced based on Erasmus' work on the Greek NT, there were only a handful of Greek manuscripts Erasmus could consult, and they were not all that old. When the KJV was produced in 1611, the problem persisted both in regard to the OT and the NT.

Today, we have more than five thousand manuscripts of the Greek NT, most of which have been unearthed in the past 150 years, and some of which go back to the second and third centuries A.D. We have the discoveries at the Dead Sea and elsewhere providing us with manuscripts more than a thousand years closer to the original OT source texts than the Masoretic Text, closer than we were in 1900. God in his providence is drawing us closer to himself, by drawing us closer to the original inspired text of the Bible in the modern era.

The cry *sola Scriptura* can echo today with a less hollow ring than in the past, because we now know the decisions taken by the church in the fourth century to recognize the twenty-seven books of the NT and the thirty-nine books of the OT (plus a few) were the right decisions. The canon was closed when it was recognized that what we needed in our Bibles were the books written by the original eyewitnesses, or their coworkers and colleagues, in the case of the NT, and those written within the context of the passing on of the sacred Jewish traditions of Law, Prophets, and Writings that went back to Moses, the Chroniclers, and the great Prophets of old.

While we owe our source texts to the ancient worthies who wrote things down between the time of Moses and John of Patmos, we owe our Bibles in the vernacular to our Protestant forebears—Wycliffe, Luther, Tyndale, Calvin, and others. Perhaps since we recently celebrated the five-hundredth anniversary of the German Reformation, it is time to say, without Protestantism, we might *not* have Bibles in all of our hands, in all of our languages. Thank God for the cry *semper reformanda*, which still rings true today.

Underlying such a cry is a profound belief that *nothing can be theologically true that is historically false*, if we are talking about theological statements *based* on some historical claim (e.g., the resurrection of Christ from the dead, or even the Donation of Constantine). The salvation history, theology, and ethics of the Bible are inexorably intertwined in many ways and places, and it will not do to try to construct a theology that ignores or plays fast and loose with the historical evidence, in particular the historical evidence in and of the Bible itself. The theologizing in the Bible cannot be abstracted from its narrative framework and thought world without distortion.

4

The English Reformation and John Wesley

Anglican Views of Scripture

> To candid, reasonable men, I am not afraid to lay open
> what have been the inmost thoughts of my heart. I have
> thought, I am a creature of a day, passing through life as
> an arrow through the air. I am a spirit come from God,
> and returning to God: just hovering over the great gulf;
> till, a few moments hence, I am no more seen; I drop into
> an unchangeable eternity! I want to know one thing—
> the way to heaven; how to land safe on that happy shore.
> God himself has condescended to teach the way; for this
> very end He came from heaven. He hath written it down
> in a book. O give me that book! At any price, give me
> the book of God! I have it: Here is knowledge enough
> for me. Let me be *homo unius libri* [a man of one book].
>
> John Wesley, preface to his *Standard Sermons*

While John Knox (1514–1572) conveyed the message of John Calvin and Calvin's Geneva Bible to the people of Scotland (through whom, along with the Puritans, this message and Bible came to New England in America, even on the *Mayflower*), he was not alone in doing so, for there were the English Puritans as well, such as Richard Baxter (1615–1691). These developments had transpired well before the Wesleys were even born in the eighteenth century.

The Reformed faith in Scotland during Knox's day struggled to find acceptance in the United Kingdom in general, as there were various martyrdoms of those holding these views, until finally in August 1560 Parliament officially recognized that this form of the Christian faith could be accepted and even preached by persons without fear of punishment.

The Puritans in general followed the teachings of John Calvin, with some modifications. One similarity was their view that the new covenant was indeed a renewal of the Mosaic covenant, such that while the ritual law in the OT had been fulfilled in Christ and did not need to be continued, the moral law carried over into Christian life. Sunday should be seen as the Christian sabbath, tithing should be the Christian practice, and strict adherence to the moral law, including the Ten Commandments, was expected of all Christians and should be enforced by the authorities or, failing that, by the church leaders. Not surprisingly, this sort of hermeneutic got some pushback from the king and governors, various of whom were either Catholic, like Mary Queen of Scots, or Anglican (but not Puritan) and reserved such matters of enforcement to governing officials. This sort of hermeneutic of the OT can be detected on a lesser scale in the writings of John Wesley, who was an ordained Anglican and not a Dissenter. Indeed, he was a convinced supporter of the monarchy.[1]

Of the Puritans the one who is most clearly an advocate of *sola Scriptura* is William Bradshaw (1571–1618): "The Word of

God contained in the writings of the Prophets and Apostles, is of absolute perfection, given by Christ the head of the Church, to be unto the same, the sole Canon and rule of all matters of *Religion*" (Bradshaw, *Several Treatises of Worship & Ceremonies*). John Greenwood, who was hanged in 1593 for challenging the monarchy and Anglicanism's cooperation with it, is also representative of various Puritans when he insists that the worship practices of Anglicanism are not in accord with the plain teaching of Scripture, whereas the Puritans worship God aright (e.g., without elaborate liturgy, without a fully sacramental view of the Lord's Supper, without a lot of expensive clothes, without the reading of a preset rather than extemporary prayer, and so on). Greenwood states clearly, "To do any thing in the worship of God without the testimonie of his word, is sinne; but there is no ground in the Scripture for such manner of praying, as having no witnesse of the word, whether God be pleased with them, or no " (Greenwood, *Writings of John Greenwood*).

Some Puritans argued against the preaching of the Apocrypha; for example, see Thomas Cartwright (1535–1603): "Let him that shall Preach choose some part of the Canonicall Scripture to expound, and not of the *Apocrypha*. Further in his ordinary Ministery, let him not take Postills (as they are called) but some whole booke of the holy Scripture, especially of the New Testament, to expound in order. In choise whereof regard is to be had both of the Ministers ability, and of the edification of the Church" (Cartwright, *Directory of Church-government*).

Most famous were the pronouncements of William Perkins (1558–1602): "We hold that the scriptures are most perfect, containing in them all doctrines needful to salvation, whether they concern faith and manners and therefore we acknowledge no such traditions beside the written word which shall be necessary to salvation, so as he which believeth them not cannot be saved " (Perkins, *Work of William Perkins*, 3:549–50).

As Ken Baker stresses, "Puritans felt that God had not given to the Church any gift more precious than Scripture. To neglect it would be a great insult to God, and to revere it was a sign of obedience to God. Intense veneration for Scripture, as the living word of the living God, and a devoted concern to know and do all that it prescribes, was Puritanism's hallmark."[2]

To the Puritans we also owe the stress on precisely following the exact meaning of words and studying them in their literary contexts. They provided an early version of what came to be called historical contextual exegesis.[3] John Owen (1616–1683) is probably most famous for this sort of expository approach. Rather than preaching small snippets of texts joined together in the lectionary the Anglicans used, Owen would work right through a biblical book. He is also famous for suggesting what later came to be called a mechanical dictation theory of inspiration. He says that God was so with the biblical writers and the Holy Spirit so clearly spoke to them that "as to their receiving of the Word from Him, and their delivering it unto others by speaking or writing—as that they were not themselves enabled, any habitual light, knowledge or conviction of the truth, to declare his mind and will, but only acted as they were immediately moved by Him. Their tongue, in what they said, or their hand in what they wrote, was no more at their own disposal than the pen is in the hand of an expert writer."[4]

Like Owen, William Perkins insisted that Scripture was the best interpreter of Scripture, not external sources of tradition:

> The supreme and absolute mean of interpretation is the scripture itself. . . . The means subordinated to the scripture are three: the analogy of faith, the circumstances of the place propounded and the comparing of places altogether. . . . The analogy of faith is a certain abridgment . . . or sum of the scriptures, collected out of most manifest and familiar places. The parts thereof are two. The first concerneth faith, which is handled in the Apostles' Creed. The second concerneth charity or love, which is explicated in the Ten Commandments.[5]

By the analogy of faith, he means the same thing as later John Wesley was to mean by the *analogia fidei*, namely that since the central theme of all Scripture is salvation by grace through faith, anything that appears in Scripture that does not comport with this red thread binding it together must be interpreted so as to agree with that theme or be seen as some sort of typological or figurative text that could not be taken in a literal sense.

One of the differences between the Puritans and the later Wesleys is that in the wake of the Enlightenment, much of the emphasis fell on the *individual's* relationship with God, the individual's conscience,[6] not on the corporate sense of identity or the idea that one is connected to Christ only through the body of Christ (i.e., the congregation). Each individual must respond to the gospel personally, for

God has no grandchildren, and the faith of one's parents will not save the individual in question.

When Paul says in 1 Cor 12 that believers are all baptized by the Holy Spirit into the one body of Christ, he's not talking about water baptism (see 1 Cor 1, where he says, "I thank God I didn't water baptize more of you"), nor is he talking about a person having an almost private relationship with the Lord. Yes, it is personal, but it is mediated through the body of Christ, where all equally have access to and are nourished by the ongoing work of the Spirit. Radical individualism becomes a besetting sin in the Protestant churches, especially some of the low church denominations.

In subsequent centuries, including now in the twenty-first, the fatal flaw of much of Protestantism was too weak an ecclesiology caused by too strong an emphasis on individual salvation, which eventually led to a splintering into hundreds of different Protestant denominations, whereas the fatal flaw of Catholicism, or for that matter Orthodoxy, was too little basis in detailed biblical interpretation, which allowed for all sorts of not merely nonbiblical but unbiblical practices as well as unbiblical theological and ethical ideas.

Neither of those latter traditions realized that the practices of literal priests, temples, and sacrifices was over when Christ died on the cross once for all time, once for all sins, once for all persons. The books of Hebrews and 1 Peter seem to have had little or no effect in those quarters. According to those books, the only priesthood would be the priesthood of all believers and the heavenly high priesthood of Christ. There was to be no intermediary priesthood. The Twelve were not priests, the apostles were not priests, and the Lord's Supper was not a literal transformation of bread and wine into the actual body and blood of Christ. This was the sort of protest the Reformers, the Anabaptists, and the Puritans all made against the Catholic and Orthodox Churches and their traditions to good effect.

By the same token, the Reformed, including the Puritans, did not realize that the new covenant was a genuinely new covenant, and laws and practices that were not specifically carried over into the new covenant were not binding on Christians, for instance, tithing. The ritual-law versus the moral-law distinction doesn't work as a New Testament hermeneutic. Paul is perfectly happy to use the ritual law about muzzling the ox to suggest that apostles should benefit from the work they do for the Lord.

In short, there were biblical problems with all these Christian traditions, some more, some less, if one applied not only a *sola Scriptura* rule to evaluating them but the sort of hermeneutic we see in the NT when commenting on the OT texts. And, furthermore, there are all the new teachings of Christ and the apostles, some of which quite clearly make OT practices like oaths, or food laws, among other things, obsolete. The Christian is to live by the law of Christ, not merely a modified Mosaic law, and the heart of Christ's law is the law of love, of God, of neighbor, of fellow believers, and even of enemies.[7] But what made Protestants, including the Reformers, pay more attention to the fact that the OT was originally written in Hebrew? Some interesting historical factors come into play.

While John Knox was exiled to Geneva along with others, he learned Hebrew for the purpose of studying the OT in its original language. He even purchased a Bible with Hebrew on one page and the Latin translation on the other and took it home with him, putting his name in it in 1561. This is of importance because Reformers like Calvin and Knox, and later John Wesley, recognized that to study the OT in its original language meant studying the Hebrew, *not* the LXX.

This in turn led to Protestants increasingly being concerned that their translations of the Bible into English involved the Hebrew text of the OT and the Greek text of the NT. You can see the outcome of this newfound insistence on the Hebrew of the OT (rather than either the LXX or the Latin Vulgate) when King James convened in 1604 a conference at Hampton Court to sort out all the disputes between Anglicans and Puritans over the Prayerbook (which the Puritans wanted abolished). John Reynolds, the leader of the Puritan delegation, proposed a new Bible translation, and while the king would not get rid of the Prayerbook of the Anglican Church, he accepted as a concession this call for a new English translation of the Bible, and the decree read, "A translation be made of the whole Bible, as consonant as can be to the original Hebrew and Greek . . . and only to be used in all churches in England in time of divine service."

As Alister McGrath has made clear, and I have reiterated, (1) the translators of the KJV were instructed to follow closely the earlier English translations (including, e.g., Coverdale, Tyndale) and not to simply attempt a fresh translation of the Hebrew and Greek texts; (2) they had only a few late Hebrew manuscripts, and basically they followed Erasmus' Greek NT (which in turn was based on six late Greek manuscripts); and (3) while they saw the original biblical texts as divinely inspired and true, there is no evidence that they thought their own translation work was infallible, inspired, and without error. Indeed, they knew they were standing on the human shoulders of previous translators, especially Tyndale. As previously noted, many of the famous phrases in the KJV were actually coined by Tyndale (e.g., "am I my brother's keeper," "the spirit is willing but the flesh is weak"). Indeed, it was not just printing errors but various errors that had to be corrected from the original printing of this translation in 1611.[8]

I point this out at this juncture because the claims of *sola Scriptura* by Protestants were based in part on the recognition that when language like "infallible" or "without error" was used, it referred in the first instance to the original-language texts written by the original inspired authors, *not to translations*, even the translation called the LXX.[9] But this, of course, was a faith statement since they did not have the autographs, the original texts as written by the inspired biblical authors.

Later, it came to be realized, with the rise of detailed text criticism and the discovery of thousands of more manuscripts, that this claim, properly speaking, *had to be applied* to the autographs, not least because no two later manuscripts of any considerable part of the Greek NT (or Hebrew OT) are exactly identical word for word, hence the need for figuring out the earliest readings of the text by certain rules of textual criticism, like "the reading that best explains the other readings is likely to be the earliest."

The notable thing about the Geneva Bible is it was the first to produce an OT translation *entirely from the Hebrew text*. It, like its predecessors, included the Apocrypha. And yes, the King James Bible of 1611 also included the Apocrypha, containing the Story of Susanna, the History of the Destruction of Bel and the Dragon (both additions to Daniel), and the Prayer of Manasseh.

In short, none of the major Bible translations that emerged during the German or the Swiss or the English Reformation produced a Bible of simply sixty-six books. It is true that beyond the sixty-six the other seven (or more) books were viewed as deuterocanonical, hence the term "apocrypha," but nonetheless, they were still seen as having some biblical authority.

The Protestant Bible of sixty-six books shows up as a standardized practice only in 1825, not before, when the British and Foreign Bible Society in essence threw down the gauntlet and said, these sixty-six books and no others. But this was not the Bible of Luther, Calvin, Knox, or even the Wesleys, who used the Authorized Version (i.e., the KJV).

What led to this exclusion was that Protestants had long treated the extra books as at best deuterocanonical, and some had even called them noncanonical, and there were some precedents for printing a Bible without these books. For example, there was a minority edition of the Great Bible from after 1549 that did not include the Apocrypha, and a 1575 edition of the Bishop's Bible also excluded those books. The 1599 and 1640 printings of the Geneva Bible left them out as well. De facto, though not de jure until the nineteenth century, these books were not treated as canonical by many Protestants.[10]

The one other Scottish or English Reformer we need now to give detailed attention to is John Wesley—who had plenty to say of relevance to the discussion of *sola Scriptura*. We must do so because the impact of the Methodist revival in the UK and Ireland led to a revival all over the eastern and midwestern United States and eventually to the largest sort of Protestant denomination—involving various groups calling themselves Methodist, others calling themselves Wesleyan, others called Nazarenes, still others called Holiness, and the Salvation Army itself, an offshoot of British Methodism. This cluster of non-Reformed churches was already in the nineteenth century the largest sort of Protestant Church in America.

JOHN WESLEY'S VIEWS

While Wesley's parents were born into Puritan families, they both became Anglicans by choice as adults before John and Charles were born, and their father, Samuel Wesley, became an Anglican priest. Especially since both John and Charles (born in 1703 and 1707) and the other children were instructed in the formative years by Susannah Wesley, whose approach to the Bible was much like that of the Puritans so far as we can tell, what was the view of *sola Scriptura* among the Wesleys?

It will be well to put on display first some of the famous John Wesley quotes of relevance to the discussion of *sola Scriptura*. We gave the beginning of the most famous quote at the outset of this chapter, but here is the rest of it:

Here then I am, far from the busy ways of men. I sit down alone: only God is here. In His presence I open, I read His book; for this end, to find the way to heaven. Is there a doubt concerning the meaning of what I read? Does anything appear dark or intricate? I lift up my heart to the Father of Lights: "Lord, is it not thy word, 'If any man lack wisdom, let him ask of God'? Thou 'givest liberally, and upbraidest not.' Thou hast said; 'If any be willing to do Thy will, he shall know.' I am willing to do, let me know, Thy will." I then search after and consider parallel passages of Scripture, "comparing spiritual things with spiritual." I meditate thereon with all the attention and earnestness of which my mind is capable. If any doubt still remains, I consult those who are experienced in the things of God; and then the writings whereby, being dead, they yet speak. And what I thus learn, that I teach.

—from the preface to the *Standard Sermons*

This famous quote is valuable but does not stand alone. John is talking about the one book that provides the guidance *for salvation*. He was, in fact, a man of hundreds if not thousands of books, so this quote and the one below about being a Bible bigot should not be taken to be some narrow-minded anti-intellectual attitude that the Bible is all the Christian needs to know about anything. Far from it. John Wesley personally edited a small library of fifty books that every Christian should read, and he had much bigger lists as well of approved reading. A clearer statement about the Bible in general can be found below in Wesley's preface to his *Explanatory Notes upon the New Testament*, which along with the *Standard Sermons* became required reading for Wesley's preachers once the movement really got going in the eighteenth century.

10. Concerning the scriptures in general, it may be observed, the word of the living GOD, which directed the first patriarchs also, was, in the time of *Moses*, committed to writing. To this were added, in several succeeding generations, the inspired writings of the other prophets. Afterwards, what the SON OF GOD preached, and the HOLY GHOST spake by the apostles, the apostles and evangelists wrote.—This is what we now stile the *Holy Scripture*: this is that *word of* GOD *which remaineth forever*: Of which, tho' *heaven and earth pass away, one jot or tittle shall not pass away*. The scripture therefore of the *Old and New Testament*, is a most solid and precious system of divine truth. Every part thereof is worthy of GOD; and all together are one entire body, wherein is no defect, no excess. It is the fountain of heavenly wisdom which they who are able to taste, prefer to all writings of men, however wise, or learned, or holy.

11. An exact knowledge of the truth was accompanied in the inspired writers with an exactly regular series of arguments, a precise expression of their meaning, and a genuine vigour of suitable affections. The chain of argument in each book is briefly exhibited in the table prefixt to it, which contains also the sum thereof, and may be of more use than prefixing the argument to each chapter; the division of the *New Testament* into chapters, having been made in the dark ages, and very incorrectly; often separating things that are closely joined, and joining those that are entirely distinct from each other.

12. In the language of the sacred writings, we may observe the utmost depth, together with the utmost ease. All the elegancies of human composures sink into nothing before it: God speaks not as man, but as GOD. His thoughts are very deep: and thence his words are of inexhaustible virtue. And the language of his

messengers also is exact in the highest degree: For the words which were given them, accurately answered the impression made upon their minds: and hence *Luther* says, "Divinity is nothing but a grammar of the language of the Holy Ghost." To understand this thoroughly, we should observe the *emphasis* which lies on every word; the holy *affections* exprest thereby, and the *tempers* shewn by every writer. But how little are these, the latter especially[,] regarded? Tho' they are wonderfully diffused through the whole *New Testament*, and are in truth, a continued commendation of him who acts, or speaks, or writes.

—from the preface to *Explanatory Notes upon the New Testament* (3rd American ed. [New York: D. Hitt and T. Ware, 1812], p. 10, emphasis original)

My ground is the Bible. Yea, I am a Bible-bigot. I follow it in all things, both great and small.

—from the June 5, 1766 journal entry in *The Works of John Wesley*, 22:42

Here we see what had become a very common Protestant polemic. The Bible is the sole final authority, and whatever other traditions may be valuable and useful, they are not inspired, not infallible, and not to be used as some sort of litmus test of genuine Christianity. John Wesley valued all sorts of Christian traditions highly, even from Reformed writers like Jonathan Edwards or Richard Baxter, with whom he had serious theological differences. And Wesley especially valued many of the traditions already mentioned in this study from the first three centuries of Christian history. This approach to the Scriptures can be seen not just in his tracts or notes on the New Testament but in the sermons he preached:

But the Christian rule of right and wrong is the Word
of God, the writings of the Old and New Testament;
all that the prophets and "holy men of old" wrote "as
they were moved by the Holy Ghost"; all that Scripture
which was "given by inspiration of God," and which is
indeed "profitable for doctrine," or teaching the whole
will of God; "for reproof" of what is contrary thereto; for
"correction" of error; and "for instruction," or training us
up, "in righteousness" (2 Tim. iii.16).

This is a lantern unto a Christian's feet, and a light
in all his paths. This alone he receives as his rule of right
or wrong, of whatever is really good or evil. He esteems
nothing good, but what is here enjoined, either directly or
by plain consequence, he accounts nothing evil but what
is here forbidden, either in terms, or by undeniable infer-
ence. Whatever the Scripture neither forbids nor enjoins,
either directly or by plain consequence, he believes to be
of an indifferent nature; to be in itself neither good nor
evil; this being the whole and sole outward rule whereby
his conscience is to be directed in all things.

—from the *Standard Sermons*, "The Witness
of Our Own Spirit," 1:225–26

And that this is a means whereby God not only gives, but
also confirms and increases, true wisdom, we learn from
the words of St. Paul to Timothy: "From a child thou
hast known the Holy Scriptures, which are able to make
thee wise unto salvation through faith which is in Christ
Jesus" (2 Tim. iii.15). The same truth (namely, that this
is the great means God has ordained for conveying His
manifold grace to man) is delivered, in the fullest manner that can be conceived, in the words which immediately follow: "All Scripture is given by inspiration of
God"; consequently, all Scripture is infallibly true; "and
is profitable for doctrine, for reproof, for correction, for

instruction in righteousness"; to the end "that the man
of God may be perfect, thoroughly furnished unto all
good works" (verses 16, 17).

> —from the *Standard Sermons*,
> "The Means of Grace," 1:249–50

Notice that Wesley sees the Scriptures as the infallible
source for teaching not just about theology but also especially about ethics. His own emphasis on social holiness,
good deeds, and the working out of one's salvation with fear
and trembling sets him apart from those who were antino-
mian, and even from some of those who kept waving the
sola fide banner in a way that suggested that human behavior
after conversion had little or nothing to do with salvation.

I beg leave to propose a short, clear, and strong argument
to prove the Divine Inspiration of the Holy Scriptures.
   The Bible must be the invention either of good men
or angels, bad men or devils, or of God.

1. It could not be the invention of good men or angels,
   for they neither would nor could make a book and
   tell lies all the time they were writing it, saying, Thus
   saith the Lord, when it was their own invention.
2. It could not be the invention of bad men or devils,
   for they would not make a book which commands all
   duty, forbids all sin, and condemns their own souls
   to hell to all eternity.
3. Therefore, I draw this conclusion, That the Bible
   must be given by Divine Inspiration.

> —John Wesley, "A Clear and Concise
> Demonstration of the Divine Inspiration of the Holy
> Scriptures," included in *The Works of the Rev. John Wesley*
> (London: Printed at the Conference-Office, 1812), 15:351

In matters of religion I regard no writings but the inspired. Tauler, Behmen, and an whole army of Mystic authors are with me nothing to St. Paul. In every point I appeal "to the law and the testimony," and value no authority but this.

At a time when I was in great danger of not valuing this authority enough you made that important observation: "I see where your mistake lies. You would have a philosophical religion; but there can be no such thing. Religion is the most plain, simple thing in the world. It is only, 'We love him because he first loved us.' So far as you 'add philosophy to religion, just so far you spoil it." This remark I have never forgotten since; and I trust in God I never shall.

—from a letter to William Law, January 6, 1756, in
The Letters of the Rev. John Wesley, 3:332

All scripture is inspired of God—The Spirit of God, not only once inspired those who wrote it, but continually inspires, supernaturally assists those that read it with earnest prayer. Hence it is so profitable for doctrine, for instruction of the ignorant, for the reproof or conviction of them that are in error or sin; for the correction or amendment of whatever is amiss, and for instructing or training up the children of God in all righteousness.

—from *Explanatory Notes upon the
New Testament,* 2 Tim 3.16

I am distressed. I know not what to do. I see what I might have done once. I might have said peremptorily and expressly, "Here I am: I and my bible. I will not, I dare not vary from this book, either in great things or small. I have no power to dispense with one jot or tittle what is contained therein. I am determined to be a bible Christian, not almost, but altogether. Who will meet me on this ground? Join me on this, or not at all."

—from *Sermons on Several Occasions* (1853),
"Causes of the Inefficacy of Christianity"

I read Mr. Jenyns's admired tract, on *The Internal Evidence of the Christian Religion*. He is undoubtedly a fine writer; but whether he is a Christian, deist, or atheist, I cannot tell. If he is a Christian, he betrays his own cause by averring that "All *Scripture* is not *given by inspiration of God*; but the writers of it were *sometimes* left to themselves and consequently made *some mistakes*." Nay, if there be *any* mistakes in the Bible, there may as well be a thousand. If there be one falsehood in that book, it did not come from the God of truth.

—from journal entry for July 24, 1776 in
The Works of John Wesley, 23:25

This is the way to understand the things of God; *Meditate thereon day and night*; So shall you attain the best knowledge; even to *know the only true God and Jesus Christ whom He hath sent*. And this knowledge will lead you, *to love Him, because he hath first loved us*: yea, *to love the Lord your God with all your heart, and with all your soul, and with all your mind, and with all your strength*. Will there not then be all *that mind in you, which was also in Christ Jesus*? And in consequence of this, while you joyfully experience all the holy tempers described in this book, you will likewise be outwardly *holy as He that hath called you is holy, in all manner of conversation*.

If you desire to read the scripture in such a manner as may most effectually answer this end, would it not be advisable,

1. To set apart a little time, if you can, every morning and evening for that purpose?

2. At each time if you have leisure, to read a chapter out of the Old, and one out of the New Testament: if you cannot do this, to take a single chapter, or a part of one?

3. To read this with a single eye, to know the whole will of God, and a fixt resolution to do it? In order to know his will, you should,

4. Have a constant eye to the *analogy of faith*; the connexion and harmony there is between those grand, fundamental doctrines, Original Sin, Justification by Faith, the New Birth, Inward and Outward Holiness.

5. Serious and earnest prayer should be constantly used, before we consult the oracles of God, seeing "scripture can only be understood thro' the same Spirit whereby it was given." Our reading should likewise be closed with prayer, that what we read may be written on our hearts.

6. It might also be of use, if while we read, we were frequently to pause, and examine ourselves by what we read, both with regard to our hearts, and lives. This would furnish us with matter of praise, where we found God had enabled us to conform to his blessed will, and matter of humiliation and prayer, where we were conscious of having fallen short. And whatever light you then receive, should be used to the uttermost, and that immediately. Let there be no delay. Whatever you resolve, begin to execute the first moment you can. So shall you find this word to be indeed the *power of God unto* present and eternal salvation.

—**EDINBURGH**, April 25, 1765.
from the preface to John Wesley, *Explanatory Notes upon the Old Testament* (Bristol: printed by William Pine, In Wine-Street, 1765)[11]

Randy Maddox provides us with a helpful summary of the main things to know about Wesley's views and use of the Bible:[12]

- Wesley never preached from the apocrypha, even though it was included in the KJV during his time.[13]

- The Wesleys (John and Charles) utilized a number of translations, including the Geneva Bible and Luther's German Bible.

- The Wesleys studied the Greek and Hebrew texts; they considered the primary languages more authoritative than the KJV.[14]

- Wesley firmly held that scripture was inspired; however, he believed that it was not always exact on "tangential matters" (genealogies, for example). Wesley argued that the Bible was "infallibly true." The word "inerrancy" was not in use in his time.

- Wesley believed that the inspiration of the Holy Spirit was key to understanding the Bible. "We need the same Spirit to understand the Scripture which enabled the holy men of old to write it."

- Wesley preached nearly the entire biblical canon, including extensive Old Testament preaching. Records ... show he preached from all books except Esther, Song of Songs, Obadiah, Nahum, Zephaniah, Philemon, and 3 John.

- Wesley read the Bible in conference with others. "If any doubt still remains [understanding a difficult passage], I consult those who are experienced in the things of God, and then the writings whereby, being dead, they yet speak."

- Wesley valued the writings of early Christian writers, particularly those of the first three centuries of the church.

- Wesley read the Bible in conference with the "Rule of Faith." He held strongly to the Apostle's Creed. What the historical church had spoken on certain matters (such as the Trinity) was important in his thinking.

- Wesley focused on the value and nature of creation. He believed that God wanted to redeem all of creation.

- Wesley was convinced that God's love for all of humanity was the central teaching of scripture. He described 1 John 4:19 as "the sum of the whole gospel": We love him because he first loved us. He called 1 John "the compendium of all the Holy Scriptures." He also frequently referred to Psalm 145:9: The Lord is loving to all, and his mercy is over all his works.

- Wesley's favorite passages (as evidenced by the frequency he preached from them) were 1 John, Romans, 1 Cor 13, and Matt 5–7 (The Sermon on the Mount).

- Wesley read the Bible because it was the guide to Christian belief, the guide to Christian behavior, and hope and sustenance for the believer.

This is all quite helpful, and Maddox openly cites the familiar evidence that Wesley did not think there were errors in the Bible.

The following are representative of Wesley:

- Wesley insisted to William Law, "If there be one falsehood in the Bible, there may [as well] be a thousand; neither can it proceed from the God of truth."[15]

- Similarly, Wesley rebutted Soame Jenyns, who suggested God sometimes left the writers to themselves and so not surprisingly they made some mistakes: "If there be one falsehood in that book, it did not come from the God of truth." Wesley published this response in a letter to the *Bristol Gazette*, in which he is even more direct—"I flatly deny there is one falsehood in the Bible."[16]

So far, so good. But here is where Maddox goes wrong, misreading Wesley on the genealogy in Matt 1. Here is exactly what Wesley said in volume 1 of his *Explanatory Notes upon the New Testament*:

> *If* there were any difficulties in this genealogy, or that given by St. Luke, which could not easily be removed, they would rather affect the Jewish tables, than the credit of the Evangelists: For they act only as historians setting down these genealogies, as they stood in those public and allowed records. . . . Nor was it needful they should correct the mistakes, *if* there were any. For these accounts sufficiently answer the end for which they are recited. They unquestionably prove the grand point in view, That Jesus was of the family from which the promised seed was to come. (3rd American ed. [New York: D. Hitt and T. Ware, 1812], p. 10, emphasis added)

Notice the two conditional statements introduced by "*if.*" Wesley does not say there are inaccuracies in the accounts. He also says that even if there are, they are not to be credited to the evangelists *because they are accurately quoting an account that may be inaccurate.* Now this frankly is no different from Paul quoting a Cretan writer who says "All Cretans are liars." It's an accurate quotation of someone else's exaggeration. And one could also mention the numerous times in the Bible that we have an accurate report of a lie. None of this in any way contradicts the quotes by Wesley above that the writers of the Bible only tell the truth, even when their sources may not.

And, furthermore, close attention to Wesley's *Notes* will show that he is flexible enough to allow that sometimes the biblical writers speak in a general rather than a specific way and should not be faulted for doing so. He doesn't see the paraphrasing of OT texts by NT writers as them making mistakes either. He believes they have the freedom under inspiration to adopt and adapt the OT texts. In other words, he believes that at times they are making homiletical use of the OT, not doing contextual exegesis, and to that end they sometimes paraphrase the text.

While Wesley considered the LXX in places less reliable than the Hebrew text, he does not think the biblical writers who rely on the LXX should be faulted if they were just trying to convey an idea or a general impression of the real meaning of the text and did so accurately. Furthermore, Wesley did not think that phrases like "the sun rose and the sun set" were scientific statements about the rotation of the sun or the earth. He accepted the conclusions of Copernicus, for example, and was very interested in the developing sciences of his day. He would say that sentences like that conveyed accurately the impression the phenomena made to the eye of the beholder. This is how it looked to them. There were a host of subjects Wesley did not think the Bible was teaching us about. Its main subjects were theology, ethics, history, and, of course, spiritual formation, the practice of living a holy life pleasing to God.

It would be hard to find in Wesley's voluminous writings an instance where he complains about the mistakes the biblical writer made. To the contrary, he thinks there is an explanation for what they do that does not question their veracity. As Maddox goes on to say, even the note on Matt 1 does not convey the whole of Wesley's views. "Wesley's more typical tendency was to extol how accurately the authors' words answered the impression made by God upon their mind, and to insist that interpersonal dynamics were always guided by God in an unerring direction" (cf. Wesley's NT notes on Acts 15.7).[17]

Maddox, however, is quite right that Wesley's hermeneutics involved (1) reading the entire Bible as all equally inspired, true, and trustworthy; (2) interpreting texts, including difficult ones, in light of the love of God; (3) reading the Bible under the guidance of the Holy Spirit, for it is the same Spirit that dwells in the believer that inspired the biblical writers in the first place; and (4) resisting the tendency to pit the law of the OT against the grace and forgiveness in the NT, in part because there is grace and forgiveness in the OT and law in the NT, but also because, as Wesley liked to say, "every moral command in both Testaments should be read as a 'covered promise'" (17). When God says, "You shall love the LORD your God," it means by God's grace "You will love the LORD your God"—God working in you to will and to do. Wesley would have nothing to do with those who would pit the OT against the NT, much less the notion that there was a canon within the canon, such that Christians should just strive to be "NT persons." (5) When Wesley found some differences between the science of his day and the Bible, in a balanced fashion he sought an explanation that did justice to both.[18] In fact, Randy Maddox suggests that Wesley may have been a biblical literalist—as long as the language was Hebrew or Greek and one is an expert in both. We may compare this to the later judgment of William Abraham, who suggests much the same but with some nuances.[19]

CONCLUSIONS ON WESLEY

We have spent considerable time on Wesley in this chapter because of the enormous impact the movement he began had on later Protestantism, and also sadly to show how far removed the modern United Methodist Church has come from honoring his principle of *sola Scriptura*, never mind Wesley's pronouncements about the necessity of chastity outside the context of heterosexual monogamy (on which see his tract entitled "Thoughts on Celibacy").

It appears clear to me that Wesley does not regard experience as an "authority" but that the truth of Scripture is *validated* in genuine Christian experience. When Wesley talks about "affections," he is not talking about human feelings in general; he is talking about religious affections stirred up by the Holy Spirit. It also appears clear to me that right reason and tradition, especially traditions from "primitive Christianity" in the first few centuries of church history, are valued by Wesley but are not seen as divinely inspired and immune to criticism. I also would argue that Wesley was not a literalist in the sense that everything in the Bible needed to be interpreted literally if it was metaphorical or figurative in the first place. But his default was to stick with the plain literal sense unless it was absurd and produced contradictions. He also doesn't seem to be bothered by generalizations or edited-down versions of a genealogy.

The one point I gather as a general sense of his view is though he doesn't make the distinction between what the Scripture teaches and what it touches, he would affirm it on the basis of 2 Tim 3.16's purpose statement. It is in regard to what Scripture *teaches* about theology, ethics, history, or spiritual formation that he says there are no errors in the Bible. He recognizes there are human expressions and phenomenological language (the sun rises and sets) in the Bible but that the biblical writer is simply speaking according to how things appear, not speaking scientifically. Wesley doesn't view the Bible as a science textbook given out of due season.

Finally, Wesley does believe tradition and interpreting things according to logic and right reason should be seen as having some authority, but the final authority and the only infallible one is the Bible.[20] This is what he means by being "a man of one book," particularly in regard to the doctrine of salvation. Having seen Wesley's strong statements, even late in life, about there not being errors in the Bible, it seems clear to me that Wesley would not have disagreed with the other Reformers or those who preceded them, like Wycliffe, that the phrase *sola Scriptura* was appropriate if by that one meant it was the *only final authority* by which all tradition, reason, and experience should be tested in regard to the subjects the Bible actually teaches us about.

Scott Jones, in the best study on this whole subject, concludes as follows:

> For Wesley the Bible is the supreme authority for Christian teaching, indeed for sound thinking as such. It must

be followed in preference to any other authority. Wesley holds a strong position on its inspiration; God is the author of Scripture. He understands that the very nature of God means he cannot be ignorant and cannot lie. Since Scripture is divinely authored, it cannot make mistakes. Wesley's position on infallibility is uncompromising: there are no mistakes in the Bible. Wesley sees Scripture as sufficient, clear, and whole. . . . Once the authority of Scripture is clearly affirmed, the subordinate roles of other authorities become clear. Reason, Christian antiquity, the Church of England, and experience are all important to the method of determining Christian doctrine. For Wesley, these five form a single witness to the truth when they are rightly used. Scripture's message is reasonable; it is best interpreted by the early church; its teachings are clarified by the Church of England; and its principles are experienced in the lives of believers.[21]

I have no quibble with this overall assessment, except I don't think Wesley saw experience as an authority per se. A validation of what the Scripture teaches and an assurance and inward confirmation that it is true—yes. An authority in itself, no. What is clear is that Wesley certainly believes the Bible is without error in what it teaches, but doubtless he would have some reservations about what later came to be called inerrancy in the twentieth century. He is clear that the Scriptures are clear and sufficient unto salvation. But the Scriptures do not address every imaginable important subject that a Christian may have to deal with.

And so Wesley's affirming of *sola Scriptura* doesn't mean that he sees it as at odds with the notion that reason and Christian tradition, ancient or modern, should have some *subordinate* authority in a Christian's or church's life. He doesn't see his high view of Scripture as a basis for anti-intellectualism or the rejection of reading and studying many other helpful books. All truth, after all, is God's truth, wherever one finds it, and if something is not consistent with Scripture on a subject Scripture teaches us about, then that something cannot be true.[22]

One of the more revealing things one can do in regard to these matters is notice how Wesley deals with purely pneumatic claims by some of his ministers and others he meets (the claim being "the Spirit told me . . ."). I am quite sure his reaction would be the same as mine was when a seminary student once came up to me after class to complain that he didn't know why he needed to learn all the stuff in our textbooks: "Why can't I just get up into the pulpit and the Spirit will give me utterance?" My response was, "Yes, Charlie, you can do that, but it is a shame you are not giving the Spirit more to work with."

John Wesley's view was to value spiritual guidance and experience, but those needed to be tested against God's Word, and furthermore, needed to comport with valid Christian tradition and reason expressed by the great Christian sages of previous eras. If these tests were not passed, then something was quite wrong with the claim itself. Experiences, after all, can be genuine and not morally good or in accord with Scripture. They are not good guides as to what is true. For Wesley, the Bible, while not the only authority, was nonetheless clearly the final and inerrant one. *This is important because it demonstrates that this very high view of Scripture did not depend on a Calvinistic view of biblical theology or a deterministic view of human history. Neither* sola Scriptura *nor "without error" should be called an invention of Reformed theology. It was held by early church fathers, Catholics before the Reformation, and both Calvinistic and Arminian Protestants thereafter, including in this case John Wesley. This is precisely why we have spent considerable time on Wesley's views in this chapter.*[23]

In the next chapter we must examine the reactions of major Christian thinkers to the rise of modern science and how that might affect one's views on the Bible. Then in the following chapter, we must examine the cultural currents that led us into modernity, which will provide us with a context for explaining why and how various churches have abandoned the Reformation cry of *sola Scriptura* and why various conservative Protestant Christians have reacted with the sort of inerrancy statements they have about the Bible.

5

The Rise of Modern Science and the Conservative Christian Response

> The Reformer is always right about what's wrong. However, he's often wrong about what is right.
>
> G. K. Chesterton

> The facts have been obscured by a smoke-screen of propagandist literature, beginning with the "illuminist" movement of the eighteenth century and prolonged by the "conflict between religion and science" in the nineteenth, whose purpose was to attack Christian theology in the supposed interests of a "scientific view of the world" which in fact is based upon it and could not for a moment survive its destruction. Take away Christian theology, and the scientist has no longer any motive for doing what inductive thought gives him permission to do. If he goes on doing it at all, that is only because he is blindly following the conventions of the professional society to which he belongs.
>
> R. G. Collingwood, *The Idea of History*
> (rev. ed.; Oxford University Press, 1993), 255–56

None of the Reformers could have foreseen what was to happen in the nineteenth and beginning of the twentieth centuries in regard to modern science. They knew nothing of Darwin's theory of evolution, nor of the study of the speed of light, nor of the theory of relativity, nor of modern geology, nor of the study of bacteria, viruses, or the atom itself.

Bishop Ussher (1581–1656), the primate of the Irish Church between 1625 and 1656, in 1650 issued his pronouncement, in a book entitled *The Annals of the Old Testament*, that according to his calculation the world began in October 4004 B.C. In fact, he was prepared to say that the first day of creation was October 23 (calculations he made on the basis of the Julian calendar). Why did he do this? There had been a long debate among Christians about the age of the earth, and before he passed away, he hoped to settle the debate, at least for his own parishioners in Catholic Ireland.

Before one dismisses Ussher as being rather like a modern fundamentalist, it should be noted that others, including scientists, had previously made similar estimates: for example, the Venerable Bede, the father of English church history, had estimated it began in 3952 B.C. Johannes Kepler estimated 3992 B.C., and Isaac Newton, who was a devout Christian, estimated the world was about 4000 years old in his own day, based on his reading of the genealogies in the OT and NT. Of course, the problem is that those genealogies are not exhaustive,[1] and in the case of Jesus' genealogies in Matt 1 and Luke 3, they are segmented and, particularly in the case of Matt 1, deliberately selective, providing a schema to show that Jesus was the perfect seven (the seventh son of the seventh son of the seventh son, etc.), the perfect descendant of King David. *These genealogies were meant to show pedigree, not list all ancestors*, which is why John Wesley made the comment he did about Matthew 1 (see above).

Once Darwin (1809–1882) had published his theory of evolution (and at that stage it was no more than a theory) and revised it under criticism as he went along, the reaction by conservative Christians ranged from outrage and out-right rejection to more moderate responses, depending on one's attitude toward science, which was growing in knowledge and importance, especially in the West. One of the most interesting responses in the nineteenth century was that of the eminent New Testament scholar J. B. Lightfoot (1828–1889), and it will be worth dwelling on his response for a bit. Lightfoot had been a professor for many years at Cambridge before he became the bishop of Durham, and he was most certainly the most formidable NT scholar of his day in the English-speaking world. Not merely a linguist or an exegete, he was also an excellent historian, and one who kept abreast of current intellectual trends of his day. Not surprisingly then, he had something to say about Darwin's theory.

Lightfoot believed fervently that all truth was God's truth wherever it came from, and he saw no fundamental reason to pit faith in the biblical witness against either science or objective historiography. He did not have an allergic reaction to the theory of Darwin as we shall see, unlike others who immediately saw it as a threat to Christian faith. He is worth quoting in full, especially considering *when* he was writing.

In 1881, presiding over the Church Congress in Newcastle, he has this to say:

> In this commemoration we are reminded of the revolution in the intellectual world which has taken place in our own time, as in the other, our attention was directed to the revolution in the social and industrial world. Here again we are confronted with a giant force, of which the Church of Christ must give an account. If we

are wise we shall endeavour to understand and to absorb these truths. They are our proper heritage as Christians, for they are manifestations of the Eternal Word, who is also the Head of the Church. They will add breadth and strength and depth to our theology. Before all things we shall learn by the lessons of the past to keep ourselves free from any distrust or dismay. Astronomy once menaced, or was thought to menace, Christianity. Long before we were born the menace had passed away. We found astronomy the sworn ally of religion. The heresy of the fifteenth and sixteenth centuries had become the orthodoxy of the nineteenth. When some years ago an eminent man of science, himself a firm believer, wrote a work throwing doubt on the plurality of worlds, it was received with a storm of adverse criticism, chiefly from Christian teachers, because he ventured to question a theory which three centuries earlier it would have been a shocking heresy to maintain. Geology next entered the lists. We are old enough, many of us, to remember the anxiety and distrust with which its startling announcements were received. This scare, like the other, has passed away. We admire the providential design that through myriads of years prepared the earth by successive gradations of animal and vegetable life for its ultimate destination as the abode of man. Nowhere else do we find more vivid and striking illustrations of the increasing purpose which runs through the ages. . . . Our theological conceptions have been corrected and enlarged by its teaching, but the work of the Church of Christ goes on as before. Geology, like astronomy, is fast becoming our faithful ally. And now, in turn, Biology concentrates the same interests, and excites the same distrusts. Will not history repeat itself? *If the time should come when evolution is translated from the region of suggestive theory to the region of acknowledged fact, what then? Will it not carry still further*

*the idea of providential design and order? Will it not reinforce
with new and splendid illustrations the magnificent lesson of
modern science—complexity of results traced back to simplicity of principles—variety of phenomena issuing from unity of
order—the gathering up, as it were, of the threads that connect
the universe, in the right hand of the One Eternal Word? Thus,*
we are reminded by these two celebrations of the twin
giants, the creation of our age, with which the Church of
Christ has to reckon—foes only if they are treated as such,
but capable of being won as trusty allies, by appreciation,
by sympathy, by conciliation and respect.[2]

Lightfoot reasoned that if God indeed incarnated himself in
history, then the clear and honest study of history is fundamental to both the understanding and the defense of Christianity. He puts the matter as follows in his unpublished
Greek Testament lecture notes for the Lenten term in 1853:

The timidity which shrinks from the application of
modern science or criticism to the interpretation of
Holy Scripture evinces a very unworthy view of its
character. If the Scriptures are indeed true, they must
be in accord with every true principle of whatever
kind. It is against the wrong application of such principles and against the presumption that pushes them too
far that we must protest. It is not much knowledge but
little knowledge that is the dangerous thing, here as
elsewhere. From the full light of science and criticism
we have nothing to fear.[3]

What Lightfoot presupposes again and again is that the Bible
is both historically and theologically, as well as ethically,
true, and whatever truth we find from some other branch of

knowledge will not threaten those truths, not least because they come from God's general revelation of truth of all kinds through his creation, and through the diligent study, exploration, investigation, and experimentation of human beings.

Needless to say, he was critical of any sort of anti-supernatural bias brought to the scientific enterprise by some of its practitioners, and he could not have foreseen how increasingly over time there would be reasons to object to science overstepping its bounds at the level of both presuppositions and experimental practice. Nor could he have foreseen how some Christians would overreact (and continue to do so). For example, he could not have seen how the fundamentalist-modernist controversy would cause some explosions in the world of Western Christianity, especially in America, where there was, as H. L. Mencken would call it, "the Scopes Monkey Trial" in Tennessee in 1925. This involved the prosecution of a criminal action brought by the state of Tennessee against high school teacher John T. Scopes for violating the state's Butler Act, which prohibited the teaching of evolution in public schools. As C. K. Barrett once remarked to me, well-educated Christians in America look over their shoulders and see a fundamentalist overreaction to science, and it affects their preaching, teaching, and practices, either positively or negatively. This was and is especially true in the American South after the Civil War. We will have more to say about this in the next chapter.

G. K. Chesterton (1874–1936) is another Christian intellectual from only a few decades after Lightfoot who also thought deeply about science and evolution, and who did not see evolution as necessarily an inherent challenge to

Christian faith or the authority and truth telling of the Bible. About science he says the following: "Evolution is either an innocent scientific description of how certain earthly things came about; or, if it is anything more than this, it is an attack upon thought itself. If evolution destroys anything, it does not destroy religion but rationalism."[4] He adds, "All science, even the divine science, is a sublime detective story. Only it is not set to detect why a man is dead; but the darker secret of why he is alive."[5]

Chesterton was a staunch defender of the Roman Catholic approach to Christianity, and he did not mince words when it came to his critique of Protestantism and its misuse and misappropriation of the Bible: "The Protestants, in separating the Bible from the Church, turned the Bible against the Church. Forgotten was the fact that it was the Church that gave us the Bible. Forgotten was the fact that the Bible was, and still is, a Catholic document. Forgotten, too, was that the Protestant Bible is an abridgement of the Catholic Bible. The Reformers discarded several books and relegated them to the category, 'Apocrypha,' which means doubtful. Doubt, the opposite of faith. The chaos in the modern world did not come from Christendom but from the disruption of Christendom [i.e., the Reformation]." The problem with this critique, of course, is (1) it was *not* the Roman Catholic Church that gave us these books; it was the original apostles, eyewitnesses, and their coworkers, most of whom were Jews and would not recognize the form of the church Chesterton is talking about; (2) these twenty-seven books were already viewed as, preached on, and taught as Scripture before the NT canon was formed; and (3) the Council of Nicaea, which led to the production of the great codexes, which in turn led to the pronouncements in the East and West and South that these twenty-seven books were the Christian Scripture, was not run by popes or the church in Rome. Indeed, the councils were held in Turkey, and the majority of the discussion involved the Greek texts, and the creeds that resulted were in Greek in the first place. The Latin representatives came to these ecumenical councils, but they do not seem to have represented even the majority of those present.

Chesterton believed in the inspiration and authority of the Bible, but he also believed what he says above, that the church had the authority and the duty to explain to all Christians the meaning of the Bible. He affirms the magisterium in this regard. Like Lightfoot, he could not have foreseen what was coming even to the Catholic Church and tradition, namely Vatican II. Today, interestingly enough, it is Evangelical Protestant scholars and conservative Catholic scholars who most often agree on the final authority of Scripture and also on the meaning of most of its texts.

Chesterton failed to recognize that the church simply *recognized* the NT canon, the books of which were already viewed as Scripture. The church did not form the canon, and so the church in the West in particular, the Latin-speaking church, cannot claim that it was the final authority rather than the Scriptures, not least because the church in the West or the East had *nothing to do with the formation of the OT Hebrew canon, the largest portion of the Bible. That was the work of early Jews.* And, frankly, after Jerome, it was finally realized that the use of the LXX was not sufficient to getting back *ad fontes* to the original inspired Hebrew text of the OT.

One further Englishman is worth mentioning in this discussion, namely C. S. Lewis (1898–1963). Because of his enormous influence even now on conservative Christians of all sorts, it is worth spending time on his views on the Bible and other relevant topics. He was not afraid to comment on the BBC or in public on any topic he was knowledgeable about, including science, for instance:

> We must sharply distinguish between Evolution as a biological theorem and popular Evolutionism or Developmentalism which is certainly a Myth. . . . To the biologist Evolution . . . covers more of the facts than any other hypothesis at present on the market and is therefore to be accepted unless, or until, some new supposal can be shown to cover still more facts with even fewer assumptions. . . . It makes no cosmic statements, no metaphysical statements, no eschatological statements.[6]

Lewis stresses that science works with empirical data and by experimentation. The very methodology does not equip it to answer ultimate questions like, Why is there something rather than nothing? Or is there a God? God cannot be experimented on.

As for his view on the authority and inspiration of the Bible, many Evangelicals who affirm *sola Scriptura* and even inerrancy today would not be on board with various things that Lewis said about the Bible. For example, "The ultimate question is whether the doctrine of the goodness of God or that of the inerrancy of Scripture is to prevail when they conflict. I think the doctrine of the goodness of God is the more certain of the two. Indeed only that doctrine renders this worship of Him obligatory or even permissible."[7] This letter comes from near the end of Lewis' life (he was to die a few months later) and reflects his considered judgment of a lifetime.[8]

In his reflections on the Psalms, he says this: "The human qualities of the raw materials show through. Naïvety, error, contradiction, even (as in the cursing Psalms) wickedness are not removed. The total result is not the 'Word of God' in the sense that every passage, in itself, gives impeccable science or history. It carries the Word of God; and we (under grace, with attention to tradition and to interpreters wiser than ourselves, and with the use of such intelligence and learning as we may have) receive that word from it not by using it as an encyclopedia or an encyclical but by steeping ourselves in its tone or temper and so learning its overall message."[9]

Now the problems with Lewis' way of looking at those Psalms are several. First, even Martin Luther long ago rightly said that what we find in the Psalms is a true revelation of the human heart in numerous places, and in some cases a human heart at odds with the heart and the will of God. The sheer honesty of Scripture again and again has this character—it not only tells us truly the will and character of God; it also opens our eyes to the sin and wickedness of the human heart, with the Psalms again and again being the clearest place this is true. Furthermore, the Bible was never intended to teach us modern science out of due season. Its focus is on salvation history, the human dilemma, the character of God, and the like. Complaining about the Bible not giving us impeccable science or modern historiography can only be called yet another example of the sin of anachronism—reading the Bible as if it were written today, rather than in its own contexts and situations. Again, the distinction between what the Bible actually teaches (namely theology, ethics, salvation history, spiritual formation) and what it touches (reflecting all sorts of human thoughts and assumptions) is a key to understanding the Bible.

But let us consider another of Lewis' relevant quotes. Interestingly, Lewis takes a decidedly incarnational approach to the nature of Scripture: "For we are taught that the Incarnation itself proceeded 'not by the conversion of the godhead into flesh, but by taking of (the) manhood into God'; in it human life becomes the vehicle of Divine life. If the Scriptures proceed not by conversion of God's word into a literature but by taking up of a literature to be the vehicle of God's word, this is not anomalous."[10] In another place he puts it this way:

> The same divine humility which decreed that God should become a baby at a peasant-woman's breast, and later an arrested field-preacher in the hands of the Roman police, decreed also that He should be preached in a vulgar, prosaic and unliterary language. If you can stomach the one, you can stomach the other. The Incarnation is in that sense an irreverent doctrine: Christianity, in that sense, an incurably irreverent religion. When we expect that it should have come before the World in all the beauty that we now feel in the Authorised Version we are as wide of the mark as the Jews were in expecting that the Messiah would come as a great earthly King.[11]

In other words, Lewis draws an analogy between the surprising nature of the incarnation of Christ himself and the incarnation of God's Word in rough-hewn human language, which is never fully comprehensive in revealing God. This is in some ways like the analogy of the Reformers, in particular that of Luther, about how the Bible is rather like the rough-hewn manger in which the perfect Christ was lain. The question is, how much divine condescension was involved? Did it really amount to taking up human misconceptions and errors and allowing them to represent God's truth? Most conservative Christians of any stripe would say no. God adequately and accurately revealed his Word in the words of human beings, which do not fully reveal the truth, but neither do they distort it.

David Williams, in his helpful article entitled "Surprised by Jack: C. S. Lewis on *Mere Christianity*, the Bible, and Evolutionary Science,"[12] chronicles how Lewis did not have a problem with the idea that the Bible contains some myth and legend, particularly in the early chapters of the OT, and he would appear to be a person who saw God as the providential divine guider of the evolutionary process, though it is difficult to pin down whether he was more in the theistic evolution camp or in the intelligent design camp. Partly, his view depends on his theology of God at some juncture in the process changing prehistoric humans into persons in the image of God by means of the addition of a soul. The problem with this whole approach is (1) the Bible doesn't subscribe to the Greco-Roman notion of an immortal soul that could be added to a preexisting human form; (2) what the story actually says is that humans were *created* in God's image, and the verb in question does not mean "refashioned." Indeed, it is a verb only predicated of God in the Hebrew text, because only God truly could create something from nothing. (3) Then there is the issue of whether Adam and Eve were historical persons, as both Jesus and Paul seem clearly to have believed. On this last point, it would appear that Lewis would agree. David Williams recounts an interesting conversation C. S. Lewis once had with Helen Gardner, an expert in English literature, at a dinner party in his home, which he found reference to in a piece written by John West. Here is the exchange as reported by Williams:

> While Lewis may not have publicly argued for the historicity of Adam and Eve, his private opinions might have been another matter. In his recent essay "Darwin in the Dock," John G. West has argued that, regardless of what he said in print, Lewis *privately* "embraced the literal existence of Adam and Eve." West chiefly bases his argument for Lewis's private belief in a literal Adam and Eve on an anecdote involving one of Lewis' Oxford colleagues, Helen Gardner, recounted in A. N. Wilson's *C. S. Lewis: A Biography*. Upon being asked at a dinner party whom he would most like to meet after death, Lewis replied, "Oh, I have no difficulty in deciding. . . . I want to meet Adam." Gardner, it is reported, replied by saying that "if there really were, historically, someone whom we could name as 'the first man,' he would be a Neanderthal ape-like figure, whose conversation she could not conceive of finding interesting." Lewis, we are told, gruffly responded, "I see we have a Darwinian in our midst" and never invited Gardner to dinner again.[13]

While Williams goes on to theorize that Lewis objected to Gardner's remark not because of an affirmation of evolution but because she saw primitive human beings as mere brutes that we would not recognize as human beings created in God's image, this I found not entirely correct. Williams goes on to report that Lewis elsewhere said, "*We do not know how many of these creatures God made*, nor how long they continued in the Paradisal state. But sooner or later they fell."[14] Notice that Lewis is not denying that there were such creatures that God made; he is simply hypothesizing that God made a variety of them, of which Adam and Eve presumably would have been representative. Notice as well that he reckons with a historical fall of human beings, whenever that happened.

One thing that Lewis does not take into account in any of his discussions of these sorts of matters, so far as I can tell, is that the Bible, while it certainly can address all human beings in all ages, is not *about* all human beings in the main. It is the story of God's people from start to finish, and other people, say the Philistines or the Romans, come into the picture only insofar as they intersect with the story of God's people. The story of Adam and Eve is in the main the story of where God's people came from, though Paul depicts Adam as the federal head of the race, whose actions affected all who came after him.[15] Even the primeval Genesis account itself makes clear there were other human beings on the planet at the same time as Adam and Eve, persons who could become wives for Cain and Abel, for example. On the other hand, Lewis doesn't seem to have a problem with the idea that human beings evolved from earlier creatures, so long as God at some point in the process transformed some of them into people in God's image. At that point the legendary story in Gen 1–2 takes on flesh and becomes fact, according to Lewis.[16]

Part of the problem in envisioning a Neanderthal Adam is that the story in Genesis reflects a time when crops were being grown and animals raised (noting the activities of Cain and Abel), in other words much later than when the protohumans seem to have lived upon the earth. In other words, we are not talking about prehistory in those stories; we are talking about ancient history, say 10,000–8000 B.C., and we now have clear evidence in southeastern Turkey, at Gobeckli Tepe and elsewhere, that in that very time range humans were already building worship sites on high places. Humans were already in the image of God back then and inherently religious.[17]

Lewis, like both Chesterton and Lightfoot before him, affirmed the value of church tradition as an authority, but not one equal to Scripture. Unlike Chesterton, he would not agree that the final authority lies with the church. In this sense Lewis, like Lightfoot, was a genuine Protestant, and his position would be something like *prima Scriptura* as the final authority on topics it actually teaches about, but not *sola Scriptura*. The radical side of the German Reformers and Luther's successors, including various Anabaptists and others, he would not agree with on this matter.

Perhaps the most fundamental problem with Lewis' approach to the Bible is his assumption that its inspiration is like the inspiration of other great literature, and so the degree of inspiration varies from place to place, book to book.[18] In other words, he looks at the inspiration in a work like Dante's *Divine Comedy*, or Milton's *Paradise Lost*, or Bunyan's *Pilgrim's Progress*, or other great literature that is not specifically Christian in character and reasons the Bible is like that. He denies plenary verbal inspiration.

The major problem with this is that 2 Tim 3.16 can be read distributively, namely "every single Scripture is God-breathed." It is not claiming that mere human inspiration of any literary sort is what produced the Bible. It is claiming it is God's Word from start to finish. This does not tell us *how* these texts were inspired, and it does not require some sort of dictation theory for every single verse, though it's clear to me that sometimes prophecy came to the seer that way—he simply listened and spoke or wrote. Lewis, however, is quite right that there is a broad range of ways to express biblical truth, and it can't simply be reduced to a series of propositions. Parables, for instance, convey truth through literary fictions, not by making abstract truth claims or constructing syllogisms.[19]

AND SO?

All three of these great Christian writers would not quibble with a phrase like *prima Scriptura*, though Chesterton would not necessarily take that to mean final authority or norm for all things involving faith or praxis. He believed in the pope's right to make doctrine into dogma by some ex cathedra pronouncements, even though only one was made in the twentieth century and only one in the nineteenth century, and both were about Mary. In fact, these are the only two such pronouncements by a pope *ever*—Mary's

Immaculate Conception (declared by Pope Pius IX in 1854 and grandfathered in after the First Vatican Council's declaration of papal infallibility in 1870) and her bodily assumption into heaven (declared by Pope Pius XII in 1950). Notice that both pronouncements came before Vatican II, which irrevocably changed the scope and manner in which faithful Catholics could approach, study, and use the Bible. One wonders what Chesterton would say now in light of faithful Catholic scholarship on the Bible in the past fifty or so years.

Clearly, much more needs to be said on these sorts of subjects, and in the next chapter we will address a few of these issues, especially vis-à-vis the question of how much authority for the Christian life tradition, reason, and experience came to be viewed as having in the second half of the twentieth century and into the twenty-first century. This must include examining the responding Evangelical faith statements about inerrancy.

6

The Modern Quadrilateral, Inerrancy, and the Overruling of Scripture

> We have turned justice into oppression, beauty into
> kitsch, freedom into license, truth into fake news,
> power into bullying. We have turned spirituality into
> self-exploration or self-gratification. We have made the
> calling to relationships the excuse for exploitation. All
> these, from a Christian point of view, have the word
> "idolatry" hanging over them.
>
> N. T. Wright, *History and Eschatology*[1]

The study of the intellectual history of the West requires taking account of the effect of the Enlightenment not merely on the church and its approach to the Bible but also on science, which increasingly became an enterprise that was separated from both the study of history and consequently the study of historical religions and involved the abandoning of the sort of religious presuppositions one finds in early scientists such as Galileo, Copernicus, and Newton, and only sometimes in more recent scientists like Francis Collins or David Wilkinson.[2]

In his excellent recent Gifford Lectures, N. T. Wright attempts to reintroduce Jesus back into the discussion of natural theology and other related subjects to good effect. One of the recurrent themes I picked up in *History and*

Eschatology is the stress on God's continued and constant involvement in his creation, and in human history for that matter, especially in the history of his people, but with a very cautionary word about trying to read off "God's will," much less God's judgments, from natural disasters like the recent pandemic.

The Bible is surely no advocate of a deistic or watchmaker deity that merely observes the world or has wound it up and left it to its own devices, nor does the Bible operate with dualistic categories like natural versus supernatural. But those very categories have been with us since at least the Enlightenment and have not merely led to "stay in your lane" kinds of discussions but have fenced off religion from the discussion of nature, even human nature. We will begin with some analysis of this important study, followed by a few excerpts from my dialogue with Tom Wright about it.

One of Tom's opening salvos exposes the ancient roots of modern dichotomies and dualisms:

> Deists and Epicureans share the view, which has now become widespread in Western culture, that there is a great gulf between God (or the gods) and the world we live in. . . . For the Epicureans, at least, the gods are made of atoms just like everything else, so they are the same *sort* of creatures as we are, only completely separated from us. This contrasts with the mainstream view of Jews and Christians, and I think for Deists as well, for whom the referent of the word "God" is different in *kind* from us, as well as in *location*, since God is believed to inhabit a different kind of space from ours, though one which overlaps and interlocks with ours. . . . For the Deist, there is one God who made the world, the

supreme watchmaker who set the machine running and keeps it well-oiled. . . . For the Epicurean, however, the gods have nothing to do with making the world, and they have nothing to do with its maintenance. . . . For some Deists at least, God cares how we behave, and may eventually call us to account. For Epicureans—and this has always been its main attraction . . . the gods don't care, and they won't judge, so how we behave is up to us, and death dissolves us into nothingness.[3]

Wright goes on to chronicle how these related worldviews (related in that they want to evacuate or eliminate divine *interference* from the natural world and the world of human history) have shaped subsequent intellectual movements in the West, kicking into high gear from the Enlightenment on. He stresses, "All these things go together: politics without God, science without God, economics without God, history without God, and finally Jesus without God. All of them take for granted a kind of über-Reformation: against the corruption, not only of the mediaeval church, but of 'the church' in general, and traditional Christianity as a whole. All these movements studied the world, and acted in the world, on the assumption that the world makes itself as it goes along, without divine interference." He goes on to cite Hume's critique of "miracles": "The mood of the times was with him. Ever since, anyone in the Western world who believes in 'miracles' has been swimming upstream."[4] In short, the development of the Enlightenment involved a revival of Epicureanism.

But the Enlightenment was also to give birth to a new idea—the notion of *progress* in human history, paralleled by the notion of upward evolution in Darwinian approaches to the origin and development of living things. This led to strange phrases like "you want to be on the right side of history," as if history had a mind of its own, purposes of its own, and was developing towards a goal. But human history is not subject to the same forces as nature. If studying history tells us anything, it is that empires rise and fall, ideas rise and fall, trends come and go, and *the notion of inevitable inherent progress toward some utopia is a myth*, although often one embraced with religious fervor. At this point global climate change is more likely to lead to the exclamation "après moi, le déluge." That's hardly progress. This part of the discussion ends with Tom's affirmation that love is a means, indeed, the most intimate means of knowing the Other, a means ruled out by the Enlightenment, which sought dispassionate "objectivity." Love overcomes the false polarization between objective and subjective and between the idealist and empiricist worldviews.[5]

The notion, as Tom says, of a God who periodically intervenes and interrupts the natural processes that it is supposed he set up in the first place is problematic. Intervention implies regular absence, but the God of the Bible is said to be, among other things, omnipresent, and as Jesus was to say, "He is always working." So the modern notion of God as an absentee landlord simply isn't a picture of God the Bible agrees with. Furthermore, what sense does it make to suggest that God sometimes works against the very "natural laws" he set up in the first place?

There is something fundamentally wrong with the natural versus supernatural distinction, if by that one means a world of pure natural causation that God occasionally interrupts. This attempt to marginalize God is said in Tom's second main chapter to parallel the attempt to marginalize Jesus and the Gospels in the discussion of what is real and how the world works. Wright puts it this way: "The challenges of Reimarus (that Jesus was a failed Jewish revolutionary) and of Schweitzer (that Jesus was a failed end-of-the-world visionary), though interestingly incompatible, were enough to generate the negative 'assured result' that the Gospels had got it wrong. Jesus was not after all what he had been made out to be."[6]

What follows in this chapter is a detailed deconstruction of these sorts of notions about Jesus and the Gospels, including a demonstration that Jesus did NOT set a timetable for the end of all things, nor for that matter was Jesus a failed (nonviolent?) revolutionary. There is no angst in the NT about a "delay" in the return of Christ: delay implies a certain date that has been postponed, but there is no date set for the parousia in the NT. The only date setting is about how the temple-centered world of early Judaism was going to be dismantled within a biblical generation. And that is exactly what happened in 70 A.D., forty years after the death of Jesus. So, Wright argues, "the idea of the literal and imminent 'end of the world' as a central belief of first-century Jews, including Jesus and his early followers, is a modern myth."[7] Just so. We should have exorcised Schweitzer's ghost from NT studies a long time ago.[8] None of the NT is predicting the end of the space-time continuum. Indeed, as Wright stresses, what it is predicted is the transformation of the mundane realm into the new creation, thus ending the present state of affairs in the world.

In other words, Jesus was not a false prophet, and Schweitzer was wrong . . . as was R. Bultmann. Bultmann comes in for some heavy criticism in this chapter, and rightly so. Among other things, he had not done any serious study of the transmission of oral traditions in early Judaism or any of the interesting memory studies now available.[9] There is a trenchant critique of Bultmann's near-total failure to engage the literature of early Judaism when trying to evaluate Jesus and Paul and the NT, resorting to caricatures found in Strack-Billerbeck about works righteousness and so on. "He was continually engaged in an attempt to find a . . . genealogy of early Christian ideas in the non-Jewish world. This led him from his early interest in mystery-religions to his later heavy (and completely unhistorical) investment in Gnosticism. Neither worked—as real history."[10] In short, Schweitzer and his disciples (who still exist) and Bultmann and his disciples (including oddly the mythicists who want to maintain that Christianity developed out of some sort of Egyptian gnostic combo) have failed to engage with the real Jewish character of Jesus and his ministry, not to mention the Jewish character of Paul and his ministry.

Both German idealism and Marxist materialism assume there is a "ghost in the machine," an inner guiding force, hidden laws, so that one can not only study what has happened but what will and must happen "according to the laws of historical development." This approach to history that is sort of pantheistic in character has been called historicism—by looking at the past and present one could figure out "where

history is going" and how to be on the "right side" of it.
Wright relies on the detailed critique of such historicism
by Karl Popper, not least because Popper does not see history as deterministic.[11] But interestingly, this whole line of
thinking leads to relativism: "They believed *X* in that time
and place because of factors *A*, *B*, *C*; but of course people in
other times and places wouldn't believe it."[12] Quoting F. M.
Turner's volume on European history, Wright notes that
this line of historicist thinking leads to the conclusion, "If
all things are a product of a particular time and place and a
particular culture *or a particular stage of Absolute Spirit coming to understand itself,* then the Bible as a document must
also be similarly time-bound."[13]

Needless to say, early Christians, and Christians today,
beg to differ. Just because something is culturally condi-
tioned *does not mean it is culturally bound* or that its meanings can't be faithfully conveyed in other cultures and
times. "The early Christians lived within ongoing history
and looked for God to act within their world. But, with
the important exception of the fall of Jerusalem, they never
claimed to read God's actions off the surface of events."[14]

Wright is on target when he says that we continue to
find new sources of information about the first-century
Jewish world (think Qumran scrolls), and therefore the task
of producing a thick description of the context in which
Jesus and others operated is constantly in process. "The task
of history *is not to substitute a new construct for the texts we
possess but to understand better what those texts were saying all
along.*"[15] Ongoing historical research is particularly good at
defeating the defeaters and naysayers. To give one example,

H. Conzelmann argued that Luke's narratives in Acts 19–21 reflected a later perspective, not least because there were no Asiarchs in Paul's day in Ephesus or Miletus. Unfortunately for this view, I found, and others have found, stones with inscriptions about Asiarchs in those very places dating to the first century A.D. Conzelmann's theories about Luke's time of writing and his mistakes were wrong. A convenient fictional theory was disassembled by an inconvenient fact and truth.

Wright goes on to lay some of his most important historical cards on the table:

> Jesus' resurrection precipitated a radical mutation within Jewish understanding of history and eschatology, which then formed a new interpretative grid: Jesus' rising was interpreted simultaneously as a very strange event within the present world *and* the foundational and paradigmatic event within God's *new* creation. This points to the fundamental argument I am making throughout this book. The idea of new creation operating from within the womb of the old—perhaps we should say, from within the *tomb* of the old—makes sense, albeit new sense, within that Jewish world in which God's space, time and matter and human space, time and matter were designed to overlap and interlock.[16]

Avoiding history when we do our theology is the first step to Gnosticism. Wright then says that later traditions, dogmas, and piety have introduced distortions and mistakes in our interpretation of the key biblical texts. "That is why it simply will not do to appeal to tradition, whether dogmatic or pious. Dogma and piety alike need to submit—as the

Reformers would insist, and as even Aquinas might agree—to the original meaning of scripture itself."[17] One cannot do history from above, as in "since God is sovereign then such and such must have happened in this way." No, the theology must arise out of the analysis of what actually did happen.

In these last sentences we see not only a helpful critique of Norman Geisler's top-down approach to biblical inspiration and authority but a clear rejection of Chesterton's approach, which would make church tradition somehow an equal authority to Scripture. For N. T. Wright, while Scripture does not stand alone as a Christian authority, it is clearly the final authority, the final litmus test of whether something is true. This is saying more than just Scripture is the "main" authority. It is a claim about Scripture being the only inspired and clearly truthful and trustworthy authority for faith and practice.

So what's been wrong with natural theology since at least Bishop Butler's *The Analogy of Religion* in the eighteenth century? Wright argues as follows:

> My sense . . . is that if a "natural theology" is seeking to find the building blocks for a doctrine of God from within the present creation, then—in terms of the model I am outlining—such an attempt must be seen as trying to have the full eschaton in advance. It is attempting to leap forwards to the final moment when God will be "all in all," but without going by the cruciform route the New Testament takes to get there. Cognate with this problem is the possibility of a "natural theology" trying to discern the being and activity of God by rational enquiry alone, screening out once more the epistemology of love which, as I have insisted all along, belongs at the heart of

> true knowledge. Thus not only will rational, left-brained knowledge not be able to grasp what is already true or see the significance of the broken signposts. . . . It will also, certainly, be unable to glimpse the eschatological promise of new creation. (*History and Eschatology*, 258)

Despite all the good that came out of the Enlightenment, including the recovery of ancient sources of all kinds and an interest in their historical substance, there was a problem, as Wright notes: "Enlightenment's radical splits of cosmology and history are bound to produce false readings. . . . [I]f we think of 'history' within a 'closed continuum' of Epicurean world-development, then anything to do with 'God' must by definition be entirely separate. . . . This is one reason why Bultmann turned 'eschatology' into a metaphor for private spiritual experience."[18]

As he sums up his argument in chapter 8, Wright emphasizes,

> What counts for the whole argument—the whole biblically based, theologically oriented argument—is *new creation*. Not sceptical historiography, not existentialised eschatology, but a new creation, a rescued, renewed and transformed creation in which the first creation, the "natural" world, is not cancelled out, as though by (in the modern sense) a "supernatural" irruption or invasion, but rather rescued, put right and transformed. The point is precisely that, as well as the discontinuity implied by all those adjectives, there is also substantial and vital continuity. Whatever the Creator will do in the end, this will not cancel . . . the first article of the Creed.[19]

"At the heart of early Christian theology we find precisely the cosmological overlap of heaven and earth, and the eschatological overlap of present and future, both of them focused on Jesus and the spirit and both of them offering a vision of the world and God, and of the relation between them, which enables us to open up the modern questions of 'natural theology' in a whole new way."[20] We must learn again to think God's own thoughts about these things after them, rather than trying to reason our way up to God. Amen and amen. This gives a good sense of the drift or trajectory of Tom's argument, and why Christians face the dilemmas they do in modernity. But more can and should be said, and so here below is an important part of the dialogue I had with Tom that deals with unhelpful dualisms.

BEN: One of the real strengths of this book is that you are able to chronicle the intellectual history from ancient Epicureanism to the present and show how the dominant worldview today is not much different from ancient Epicureanism in the way it brackets out God and "the supernatural" from history and "natural causation." Since most of our audience will associate Epicureanism with hedonism, the pleasures of the palate and the flesh, explain what you mean by Epicureanism, and how it still informs modern presuppositions about the nature of the world.

TOM: Ancient Epicureanism was indeed known—by its opponents at least!—as hedonism. This, however, was at least in part a slur, since the serious Epicureans (represented by Lucretius) knew that overindulgence in fleshly pleasures was counterproductive. They recommended a cooler, more detached pursuit of pleasure.

But Epicureanism was far more than a charter for pleasure, whether licentious or restrained. It was a worldview, competing with Stoicism and the various forms of Platonism—as it still does. Stoicism saw the gods and the world as bundled up together in various kinds of pantheistic mix; Epicureanism saw the gods as completely detached from our world (though made ultimately of the same stuff), so that the gods don't interfere in our world and nothing we can do will affect them. Since there is no divine action in the world, the world "makes itself" through the random movement of atoms, which sometimes "swerve" and, bumping into one another, produce different forms of life. This is the direct ancestor of modern evolutionism (not the biological theory of evolution, but the worldview that preceded it by a century or more on the a priori assumption that, with God or the gods absent from the world, the world must proceed under its own steam). Epicureanism is therefore at the root a theory about how the world works, a theory that allows for the existence of the gods but that insists they are not involved in our world, nor we in theirs. Hedonism—in whatever form—is therefore the only proper motivation for action, since nothing we can do will either impress or affect the gods, and since when we die our atoms simply dissolve, so that, in the famous phrase, at death there is "nothing to be afraid of." As Catherine Wilson comments in her book on Epicureanism at the origins of the Enlightenment, the ancient philosophy sounds remarkably familiar because it is in fact what most modern Westerners implicitly believe. The real tragedy is that so many modern Christians have responded not by reinhabiting the biblical worldview but by reaching for forms of Platonism (including the word "supernatural" in its modern sense of divine "intervention"!) to bridge the gap between our world and God's world. How much better to explore the biblical notion of the temple and the promise—not that we will eventually dwell with God, but that God will eventually dwell with us, setting up his kingdom "on earth as in heaven."

The Platonist would be shocked: that's a category mistake, and an unwelcome one at that. The Stoic would be puzzled: surely God's world and the human world already intersected completely (ignoring the problem of evil, of course). The Epicurean would find the idea of God's kingdom arriving on earth both tasteless, tactless, and thoroughly inconvenient. One might have to start sharing one's favorite wine with those lower-class people down the road. . . . Jesus would be delighted, having already turned the local water into even better wine, but always ready to accept another bottle or two from unexpected sources.

BEN: It appears that one of your main concerns in this book is to insist that since history and historical figures like Jesus are part of the realm of space and time, what they have to say or contribute to the discussion of natural theology should not be eliminated a priori, just because that material comes from a source of revelation, the Scriptures, and so it would be a category mistake to include it. You attribute this exclusion to, among other things, the division in European thinking between the "eternal truths of reason" and the contingent truths of history, with the latter being excluded (see Lessing's ugly ditch) as not relevant, as a category mistake. Or it is excluded because the natural realm is one thing, run by natural causes, and the supernatural is something else (and is assumed by some to intervene or invade the natural realm from time to time). Why is this sort of compartmentalization of reality wrong, and what exactly is wrong with it?

TOM: This is a complex question because there were several things going on in influential eighteenth-century thought. Lessing's ugly ditch did indeed separate the eternal truths of what he called "reason" (which means, I think, that which we can figure out by pure thought working on very basic intuitions about the world) and the contingent truths of history (i.e., the messy, unpredictable, and apparently random happenings in the world). This appears to be a diminution of history—that is, we can try to do it but we know it won't get us anywhere with the biggest questions of all. Equally, however, the same split functioned the other way, as when reductionist "historians"—Hume in Scotland; Reimarus, published by Lessing himself, in Germany!—who said in effect "we will do the history"—in Reimarus' case, the history of Jesus—"and we'll show that your Christianity is based on lies, deceit, misunderstandings, and mistakes." Behind this, yes, there was of course a Platonic split in which the world of space, time, and matter, even if in its own way beautiful and well-made in some respects, was still essentially secondary, and one should turn from its fleeting shadows to pursue the "forms," the reality itself. And so it goes . . . all the way through D. F. Strauss to Bultmann and his followers—though, as I stress in the book, they were at least trying to recover genuine early Christian faith, whereas they were "retrieved" in the English-speaking world in terms of a translation into positivism (the search for "facts" and the "discovery" that there weren't too many of them to be had). These massive confusions have bedeviled the discipline of NT studies ever since and have made it seem to theologians as though "nothing good will come of history"—which merely reinscribes Lessing's ditch. And so it goes.[21]

What we should certainly learn from this sort of discussion is that many factors have led to differing ways to discuss the issue of the Scriptures and their inspiration and authority. *And what we also should realize is that various of these intellectual trends have most certainly led to an erosion even within the church of a clear and consistent affirmation of the inspiration, the authority, and the truth of Holy Scripture.* As a case study we may consider what has happened to a denomination like the United Methodist Church, which has in recent days become the "Untied" Methodist Church, with thousands of churches leaving the denomination. To understand what has happened we must go back to the beginning of the discussions about the so-called Quadrilateral.

WHEN THE QUADRILATERAL BECAME AN EQUILATERAL

The discussion began in United Methodism in the 1960s, not long after the merger between the Methodist Episcopal Church and the Evangelical and United Brethren. Initially, the discussion took a historical focus on what John Wesley himself thought about Scripture, tradition, reason, and experience. This was summed up in various ways, and frankly in ways that were at odds with what we have already seen John Wesley thought about the final authority and truthfulness of Scripture. In his view, in disputes between tradition and Scripture, or reason and Scripture, or experience and Scripture, Scripture only was to have the last and deciding word. These other three factors were to be defined and normed by Scripture. This helps explain the summaries one finds below.

In the first place, Albert Outler, one of the greatest Methodist historians and theologians, had coined the term "Quadrilateral," and much later wished he had never done so, as it opened Pandora's box to all sorts of formulations that amounted to either tradition or reason or experience trumping what the Bible said about some subject.[22] Here are some of the subjects under consideration at the initial stage of the discussions about these other "authorities." (Though it should be noted from the outset that Outler quite rightly did not think Wesley talked about experience as an "authority" for Christian life, nor did Outler think that was the right way to frame the question. Rather, it was framed as follows: "The United Methodist Church asserts that 'Wesley believed that the living core of the Christian faith was revealed in Scripture, illumined by tradition, vivified in personal experience, and confirmed by reason. Scripture [however] is primary, revealing the Word of God "so far as it is necessary for our salvation.""[23]) What is not said here is what authority the Bible has when it addresses issues other than soteriology.

For Wesley, Scripture alone is the foundation for the core of true religion, but tradition and reason are to be valued. Wesley did not think that the value of church tradition weakened over the course of time; indeed, he especially valued the church fathers and traditions of the first three centuries, which he regularly called primitive Christianity, which Christians of his own day needed to embrace and emulate. He did not buy the notion that truth was time sensitive or that true traditions waned in authority as time passed. This would be like saying the Bible or church tradition is true and valuable on Monday, but not later in the week. The passage of time has nothing to do with how true or valuable something is. Wesley might even have been willing to speak about the irrelevance of relevance when it comes to such timeless traditions.

While Scripture itself is sufficient as a foundation for true religion, "of what excellent use is reason, if we would either understand ourselves, or explain to others, those living oracles!"[24] Wesley argued that without right reason we cannot understand the truths of Scripture. But Wesley cautioned that reason doesn't stand alone. It requires the assistance of the Holy Spirit to guide it in the right direction. Reason cannot produce faith or justification, but it can provide vital assistance in understanding the faith.

As for experience, Wesley did not see it as an authority in itself. He saw "religious affections" and assurance of the heart as the confirmation in personal experience of the truths that the Scriptures were teaching. Wesley was all too aware that experiences can be quite genuine and in fact not a good guide to the truth about something. He would have found very odd and very wrong claims like "I cannot deny my experience" or "my experience tells me that the Bible is wrong about this or that." No experience prompted by the Holy Spirit would do anything other than illuminate and give personal assurance about the truth in the Scriptures. Experiences *in themselves, even spiritual experiences*, are not reliable guides to the truth and, however genuine, must be carefully evaluated in light of the Scriptures.

What you see in Wesley and his successors, like Francis Asbury or Richard Watson, is that they valued tradition, right reason, and experience, but they did not see experience as a final norm or authority. Whatever authority tradition and reason might have, it paled in comparison to, and had to be normed by, the authority and truth of Scripture. While this position might not be called by some *sola Scriptura*, it could certainly be said to affirm Scripture as the final authority, the norm of other valuable thoughts and traditions.[25]

In other words, were Wesley alive today he would have seen the Quadrilateral as a modern invention, if by that one meant four rather equal sources of authority for the Christian life. I have actually heard Albert Outler say he wished he had never uttered the word "Quadrilateral" because of the way it has come to be used. I once wrote an article for the *Circuit Rider* (a defunct UM publication) where I suggested that reason, tradition, and experience were seen by Wesley as avenues into the central and infallible truths of Scripture or as means by which that central truth could be expressed—using the analogy of a hub and spokes of a wheel. But there have been other, very different modern formulations about the Scripture as not just infallible but as inerrant, and we must turn to one of these in a moment.

It was not just in Methodism that a cultural change was perceived that affected how one viewed things like *sola Scriptura* and the authority of the Bible on a host of issues. Even in very conservative denominations and independent Evangelical churches there was a strong feeling that some kind of statement needed to be made to stem the declining view of the veracity and applicability of the Bible not only in the life of the country in general but even in the life of conservative Christian churches and communities.

One of the telltale signs of decline was the rapid decline of biblical literacy in all sorts of churches, coupled in part with the decline of discipleship programs, including Sunday school. Why did that happen? The rise of praise services influenced heavily by the popularity of popular music, including soft rock music, *unintentionally* led to people, especially young people, attending a worship service just to hear the music and not staying for Sunday school or other Bible study groups. Something had to be done, and the leaders of Evangelicalism decided a major statement was in order, a statement that was first drafted in 1978 and then got two more additional parts in the 1980s.[26]

THE CHICAGO STATEMENT ON INERRANCY

This statement was put forth by some two hundred or more Evangelical leaders in October 1978 in Chicago and is detailed, going on for some six pages. Here is the essence of it.

A Short Statement

1. God, who is Himself Truth and speaks truth only, has inspired Holy Scripture in order thereby to reveal Himself to lost mankind through Jesus Christ as Creator and Lord, Redeemer and Judge. Holy Scripture is God's witness to Himself.

2. Holy Scripture, being God's own Word, written by men prepared and superintended by His Spirit, is of infallible divine authority in all matters upon which it touches: it is to be believed, as God's instruction, in all that it affirms, obeyed, as God's command, in all that it requires; embraced, as God's pledge, in all that it promises.

3. The Holy Spirit, Scripture's divine Author, both authenticates it to us by His inward witness and opens our minds to understand its meaning.

4. Being wholly and verbally God-given, Scripture is without error or fault in all its teaching, no less in what it states about God's acts in creation, about the events of world history, and about its own literary origins under God, than in its witness to God's saving grace in individual lives.

5. The authority of Scripture is inescapably impaired if this total divine inerrancy is in any way limited or disregarded, or made relative to a view of truth contrary to the Bible's own; and such lapses bring serious loss to both the individual and the Church.

Articles of Affirmation and Denial

Article I. We affirm that the Holy Scriptures are to be received as the authoritative Word of God. We deny that the Scriptures receive their authority from the Church, tradition, or any other human source.

Article II. We affirm that the Scriptures are the supreme written norm by which God binds the conscience, and that the authority of the Church is subordinate to that of Scripture. We deny that Church creeds, councils, or declarations have authority greater than or equal to the authority of the Bible.

Article III. We affirm that the written Word in its entirety is revelation given by God. We deny that the Bible is merely a witness to revelation, or only becomes revelation in encounter, or depends on the responses of men for its validity.

Article IV. We affirm that God who made mankind in His image has used language as a means of revelation. We deny that human language is so limited by our creatureliness that it is rendered inadequate as a vehicle for divine revelation. We further deny that the corruption of human culture and language through sin has thwarted God's work of inspiration.

Article V. We affirm that God's revelation in the Holy Scriptures was progressive. We deny that later revelation, which may fulfill earlier revelation, ever corrects or contradicts it. We further deny that any normative revelation has been given since the completion of the New Testament writings.

Article VI. We affirm that the whole of Scripture and all its parts, down to the very words of the original, were given by divine inspiration. We deny that the inspiration of Scripture can rightly be affirmed of the whole without the parts, or of some parts but not the whole.

Article VII. We affirm that inspiration was the work in which God by His Spirit, through human writers, gave us His Word. The origin of Scripture is divine. The mode of divine inspiration remains largely a mystery to us. We deny that inspiration can be reduced to human insight, or to heightened states of consciousness of any kind.

Article VIII. We affirm that God in His Work of inspiration utilized the distinctive personalities and literary styles of the writer.[27]

Here are the articles not found in the short form of the statement that further clarify matters.

Article IX.
WE AFFIRM that inspiration, though not conferring omniscience, guaranteed true and trustworthy utterance on all matters of which the Biblical authors were moved to speak and write.

WE DENY that the finitude or fallenness of these writers, by necessity or otherwise, introduced distortion or falsehood into God's Word.

Article X.

WE AFFIRM that inspiration, strictly speaking, applies only to the autographic text of Scripture, which in the providence of God can be ascertained from available manuscripts with great accuracy. We further affirm that copies and translations of Scripture are the Word of God to the extent that they faithfully represent the original.

WE DENY that any essential element of the Christian faith is affected by the absence of the autographs. We further deny that this absence renders the assertion of Biblical inerrancy invalid or irrelevant.

Article XI.

WE AFFIRM that Scripture, having been given by divine inspiration, is infallible, so that, far from misleading us, it is true and reliable in all the matters it addresses.

WE DENY that it is possible for the Bible to be at the same time infallible and errant in its assertions. Infallibility and inerrancy may be distinguished, but not separated.

Article XII.

WE AFFIRM that Scripture in its entirety is inerrant, being free from all falsehood, fraud, or deceit.

WE DENY that Biblical infallibility and inerrancy are limited to spiritual, religious, or redemptive themes, exclusive of assertions in the fields of history and science. We further deny that scientific hypotheses about earth history may properly be used to overturn the teaching of Scripture on creation and the flood.

Article XIII.

WE AFFIRM the propriety of using inerrancy as a theological term with reference to the complete truthfulness of Scripture.

WE DENY that it is proper to evaluate Scripture according to standards of truth and error that are alien to its usage or purpose. We further deny that inerrancy is negated by Biblical phenomena such as a lack of modern technical precision, irregularities of grammar or spelling, observational descriptions of nature, the reporting of falsehoods, the use of hyperbole and round numbers, the topical arrangement of material, variant selections of material in parallel accounts, or the use of free citations.

Article XIV.

WE AFFIRM the unity and internal consistency of Scripture.

WE DENY that alleged errors and discrepancies that have not yet been resolved vitiate the truth claims of the Bible.

Article XV.

WE AFFIRM that the doctrine of inerrancy is grounded in the teaching of the Bible about inspiration.

WE DENY that Jesus' teaching about Scripture may be dismissed by appeals to accommodation or to any natural limitation of His humanity.

Article XVI.

WE AFFIRM that the doctrine of inerrancy has been integral to the Church's faith throughout its history.

WE DENY that inerrancy is a doctrine invented by scholastic Protestantism, or is a reactionary position postulated in response to negative higher criticism.

Article XVII.

WE AFFIRM that the Holy Spirit bears witness to the Scriptures, assuring believers of the truthfulness of God's written Word.

WE DENY that this witness of the Holy Spirit operates in isolation from or against Scripture.

Article XVIII.

WE AFFIRM that the text of Scripture is to be interpreted by grammatico-historical exegesis, taking account of its literary forms and devices, and that Scripture is to interpret Scripture.

WE DENY the legitimacy of any treatment of the text or quest for sources lying behind it that leads to relativizing, dehistoricizing, or discounting its teaching, or rejecting its claims to authorship.

Article XIX.

WE AFFIRM that a confession of the full authority, infallibility, and inerrancy of Scripture is vital to a sound understanding of the whole of the Christian faith. We further affirm that such confession should lead to increasing conformity to the image of Christ.

> *WE DENY* that such confession is necessary for salvation.
> However, we further deny that inerrancy can be rejected
> without grave consequences, both to the individual and
> to the Church.

This statement was quickly supplemented in 1982 by a statement on biblical hermeneutics, and then in 1986 one on biblical application. The first of these three statements became the faith statement of the Evangelical Theological Society, and it occasionally has been used in a judicial manner to exclude some who wanted to join the society or expel some thought to not really affirm these statements. For our purposes, what is important is that this is as clear an assertion of *sola Scriptura* as one will find in the modern world, especially noting articles 1 and 2 above.

So what should we think about this statement? You will notice an almost complete absence of discussion about the authority of translations of the Bible. Furthermore, nothing is said at all about the *infallibility* of some translators or translations of the original-language texts. We must especially take note of the article that says that technically speaking, these claims about inerrancy apply to the autographs. Exactly right. But the next statement in that same article claims this: "which in the providence of God can be ascertained from available manuscripts with great accuracy. We further affirm that copies and translations of Scripture are the Word of God to the extent that they faithfully represent the original." And who decides to what extent this or that translation does faithfully represent the original? We are not told.

This seems to suggest that the committee is either dismissing or unaware that there are places in both the Hebrew OT and the Greek NT where complex textual issues still haven't been resolved because it is very difficult to decide what the original reading in the autograph was, and that being the case it is also difficult to decide how to properly translate the text in question.

The statement that no essential Christian belief is in doubt because of textual uncertainty is true but not to the point. It is one thing for a translation to be faithful, quite another for it to be infallible or inerrant. There are numerous verses where several possible translations are viable, and equally devout and conservative translators may well disagree about what the original said and meant.

And then there is the statement about science and what the Bible says about origins. Article 12 ends with this statement: "We further deny that scientific hypotheses about earth history may properly be used to overturn the teaching of Scripture on creation and the flood." In the further exposition, this statement is neither clarified nor qualified, leading one to wonder whether we are to suppose that the statement requires a particular view about the age of the earth and other related matters.

In the exposition that appears to have been originally offered by Carl F. Henry himself, the original editor of *Christianity Today*, we hear this: "Since God has nowhere promised an inerrant transmission of Scripture, it is necessary to affirm that only the autographic text of the original documents was inspired and to maintain the need for textual criticism as a means of detecting any slips that may have crept into the text during the course of its transmission." Exactly right, and Henry goes on to remind, "No translation is or can be perfect and all translations are an additional step away from the *autographa*." Just so, and so while Henry is right that we can have good confidence that we know what most of the original texts said, any such statement about the autographs in toto is a faith statement and aspirational in character. And some will say that since every translation is already an interpretation of the original language text, we can call those translations the Word of God only with some qualification, such as "this conclusion does not apply to verses where we have serious textual problems and we are very uncertain about what precisely the original text said and meant."

I personally do not have a problem signing the more abbreviated forms of these faith statements of various conservative seminaries that mention the word "inerrancy" or "infallible," so long as I get to define what counts as an error. When it comes to what the Scripture teaches about its subject matter—theology, ethics, and salvation history—I believe it speaks truthfully and is trustworthy. The remark in the Chicago Statement about "whatever the Scripture touches" doesn't reckon sufficiently with things like the use of phenomenological language, where modern scientific claims are *not* being made about cosmology, anthropology, and other such scientific topics.[28] Nor does it reckon with what we have said earlier about the Psalms revealing truthfully what is in the heart of human beings, not necessarily what is in the heart of God. Nor does it deal with reports of errors and lies made by some of the characters in Scripture.

We can say they are truthful reports about lies, but then that means that not all the things mentioned in Scripture are true in the pure sense of that term.[29]

While I think that the Chicago Statement on inerrancy was a good-faith attempt to combat some of the slippage in major denominations when it comes to the inspiration, authority, truthfulness, and applicability of Scripture to the church today, and I would not want to say that the statement dies the death of a thousand qualifications, nevertheless one could say that occasionally in places it says too much (e.g., about what the Scripture touches), and occasionally it probably says too little, actually. Nevertheless, this statement is an understandable reaction to what was going on not only in the intellectual life of the broader U.S. culture but in major denominations where the church culture was increasingly becoming more like the general culture on a host of issues (e.g., abortion).

When one looks at the list of signees of this original document, one notices three things that stand out like a sore thumb: (1) there are no women pastors or scholars among the signees; (2) almost without exception the signees are white Anglo-Saxon Protestants; and (3) I see exactly no notable Wesleyan or Methodist signees at all or African Americans either. In short, this statement is mostly made by Reformed pastors and scholars of that era, and were a similar statement to be commissioned today, it might well have very different representatives and different emphases. What would hopefully not be different is an affirmation that the Scriptures are God-breathed, are authoritative for faith and practice, and tell the truth about whatever they intend to teach us about salvation history, theology, ethics, and spiritual formation.[30]

WHY IS THE BIBLE THE WAY IT IS?

Sometimes I am asked the question—If God is omnipotent and revealed the truth without error to the original inspired authors, why did he not preserve the original texts in their transmission over many centuries such that we don't have to deal with thousands of textual variants and various attempts to reconstruct the original form of this or that verse? This is a good and fair question, and I think there are several answers. The first is straightforward—once God handed the Scriptures over to human beings in pristine form; the attempts to make copies of it involved non-inspired people who gave their best efforts but made mistakes. In other words, in the hands of uninspired fallen human beings, even those who operated in good faith were prone to mistakes of various sorts, and we know some of them even had the hubris to try to "improve" or even correct what they thought were errors in the original texts. A good example of the latter would be the anti-feminist tendencies of the Western text of Acts.[31] The editors of that textual tradition wanted to erase the evidence of women playing ministerial roles, like Priscilla along with her husband Aquila in Acts 18 teaching Apollos. This was deliberately tendentious editing.

But there was also the problem of laborious copying of texts originally written with endless streams of Greek letters, with no separation of words, sentences, and paragraphs, and no chapter and verse delineations. It was easy, far too easy, to lose one's place while copying such a text, and accidentally skip to the next line or make many other mistakes. Take a look at the following picture of a very early Christian papyrus, 𝔓⁴⁶, and you will see what I mean.

This document dates to between 175 and 225 A.D. and is one our earliest copies of some of Paul's letters, and as you can see, it is written in a continuous flow of Greek letters.[32]

But again, why would God allow such changes or corruption of the inspired text? My best answer would be *to prevent bibliolatry*—the worship of a perfect object, the Bible. When you read mythological stories about the origins of the Book of Mormon, you begin to see why God did it the way he did. The Bible did not fall from the sky on golden plates—it too went through a process of incarnation, just like the Word of God called Jesus.

It was subjected to the same limitations of time, space, knowledge, and power to which Jesus willingly submitted in order to be truly human. The Bible was in the earthly and human realm, which was fallen, and was in the hands of fallible human beings, and things happened. Fortunately for us, Jesus came to us in an unfallen condition, presumably like the autographs of the Bible, and Jesus did not give way to the temptations that various of the Bible's handlers did give way to over time. Jesus remained sinless; the transcribers and handlers of the Bible not so much, hence the ongoing need for textual criticism.

THE WAY OF ALL FLESH

But there is another factor at play here, and it is one that has unfortunately divided major Protestant denominations again and again in the past several decades, namely the rejection of what the Bible actually teaches about biblical forms of marriage and appropriate human sexual expression. Let me be clear here that we are not just talking about issues where legitimate differences of interpretation of biblical texts are possible and to be respected. No, we are actually talking about the rejection of what the Bible actually *says and teaches* about human sexuality and marriage. And this means the rejection of the final authority of the Bible in such matters. It means placing oneself and one's own judgment over rather than under the authority of Scripture. And this is a major mistake.

For example, you will hear the claim that the Bible doesn't mention homosexuality or lesbianism, or if it does it is referring to something other than modern consensual relationships between adults. Sometimes you will hear it said it is about pederasty, a form of child abuse, or sex with one's slaves, which anyone would condemn. Alas for this suggestion, it is false at both the level of history and the level of biblical interpretation. There were all kinds of sexual relationships between adults in the ANE and in the Greco-Roman world. Those biblical statements are not just about pederasty or sex with slaves or so-called sacred prostitution.

The Bible condemns grown men lying with grown men in Leviticus. In Romans 1 it clearly condemns any form of homosexual practice and even mentions lesbian sexual practices as well. It is irrelevant that the Bible doesn't use the term "homosexual" since it clearly condemns same-sex sexual activity both in the OT and the NT. It is seen as a clear violation of the created order, in which God made male and female for each other. Let's be perfectly clear that what is condemned is certain forms of sexual *behavior*. The critique is not about one's inclinations, not least because all human beings have various sorts of fallen inclinations.[33] And no one should make the mistake of saying love me, love my sexual behavior.

A person created in God's image is so much more than his or her sexual behavior, and if one defines oneself purely on the basis of one's sexual behavior or makes it a sine qua non to who they are, they have trivialized themselves. Consider on the one hand young children well before puberty or senior citizens who don't engage in sexual expression. Do we really want to suggest that they somehow have *less identity, less worth, or less fulfillment simply because they don't engage in sexual activity?* Surely not. In addition, there is a difference between loving people and loving all their behaviors or ways. The love the Bible requires of us toward all humans, whatever their flaws, doesn't require us to accept their sinful behavior, much less baptize it and call it good.

And furthermore, it is a myth that Jesus has nothing to say on these matters. Beyond cavil, in Matthew 19 Jesus tells his own disciples that either heterosexual monogamy or celibacy in singleness (called being a eunuch for the kingdom) are their *only two options*. And let me be as clear as I can be—we are not talking about (1) a rejection of one possible interpretation of these biblical texts or (2) a rejection of what Books of Disciplines in various denominations say about these texts. *No, what is being rejected here is the very authority of the Bible itself, and I would remind those who do so that the very verse that tells us that every verse in the OT is God-breathed (2 Tim 3.16) also says that one of the main purposes of the Bible is training in righteousness or holiness! At a minimum we are talking about the rejection of major biblical teaching on both human sexuality and Christian marriage.* It is folly and arrogance to say that scholars and clergy for nineteen hundred years got Jesus' and Paul's teachings on these matters wrong, but "now we know better."

And behind that rejection is an acceptance that one has a personal right to decide these matters for oneself. In short, one is asserting *one's own authority* over the authority of the Bible. In such a scenario, the individual is the final authority in such matters. This, however, is just one more reflection of where extreme individualism and narcissism leads. A telltale sign that things have gone badly wrong is when people talk about "my truth." But truth is not an individual possession, nor does it differ from person to person. Truth makes a claim on all of us, like the truth that we are all affected by gravity. I don't get to custom-make a truth that is "my truth" and applies only to me and no one else necessarily. That is not the way truth works.

And no, this is not about love, if by love one means the holy love that Jesus and the writers of the Bible sanctioned. It may be about attraction, or about inclinations, or desires, or urges, but what it is not about is holy love as defined in the Bible, a kind of love that is *not* primarily about feelings. When the Bible *commands us to love* our neighbor as ourself, it is not primarily about feelings, not least because feelings cannot be commanded.

What has happened in the wake of these changes of policy in major denominations is the loss of moral authority. Various churches have simply capitulated to the cultural trends and have lost their way, badly. The more recent ones who have literally gone the way of all flesh have not learned the lessons when other denominations earlier went in this direction—with massive losses of membership, integrity, and moral authority. It is like that old *Pogo* cartoon where one of the characters says, "I have seen the enemy, and the enemy is us." It turns out that often laypeople have better moral instincts than their modern clergy leaders do.

It is irrelevant what the culture or official policy of the land says about these matters. The culture will do what it will do, particularly if the majority of citizens in the United States or elsewhere support such non-Christian approaches to human sexuality and marriage. Clearly, for Christians, the final authority in all such matters of faith and practice should be what the Bible teaches about these things. But enough about what in the culture has prompted various Christians to reemphasize *sola Scriptura*, or at least the Bible as the final authority in all such matters. In our next and final chapter, we must consider the legacy of the idea of *sola Scriptura*, and how we should view this concept today.

7

Quo Vadis?

The Legacy and Future of *Sola Scriptura*

> Turning and turning in the widening gyre
> The falcon cannot hear the falconer;
> Things fall apart; the centre cannot hold;
> Mere anarchy is loosed upon the world,
> The blood-dimmed tide is loosed, and everywhere
> The ceremony of innocence is drowned;
> The best lack all conviction, while the worst
> Are full of passionate intensity.
>
> W. B. Yeats, "The Second Coming"

To some extent, at least in the twenty-first century, the political polarization in the general culture has spilled over into the church, particularly for those who believe the mistaken notion that the United States was founded to be a Christian nation, and that the nation at its best has always reflected Christian values, at least for the most part. In fact, various of the most influential Founding Fathers were Deists (e.g., Thomas Jefferson), and their approach to government that involved democracy and parliamentary government with elected officials is nowhere to be found in the Bible. It owes more to people like John Locke than to John son of Zebedee. But I digress.

As we draw this study to a close, what are some salient points that we must carry with us as we go forward into the twenty-first century? First of all, though *sola Scriptura* is one of the main "solas" that the Reformation was all about, it was *not* in the first place a Protestant or even Reformation idea. It existed long before Luther and Calvin and was a term used to rebut many of the unbiblical papal claims. What was meant by the term was that the Bible was the *final* authority, the litmus test on all other claims in the church about authority, even those of popes and patriarchs or councils. *What it did not actually mean before the Reformation is that the Bible was the only authority the church and Christians in general should recognize. "Orthodox" Christian tradition and praxis had some authority, as did the use of reason to understand the world and Scripture. The term was coined by Catholics upset with papal abuse of power.*

During the various Reformations things changed somewhat. Particularly in the German and Swiss Reformations, the term was sometimes taken to mean not just the final authority in all matters of faith but the *sole* real authority. Other things only had authority if they could be shown to be based in Scripture or were consonant with Scripture. The model I mentioned earlier in this study (in which tradition, reason, and experience were seen as avenues into the truths of Scriptures or vehicles out of which the truth of Scripture could be expressed) is closer to what some of the Reformers seem to have taught. It is certainly the view of John Wesley. On such a model, these other three things are not authorities in their own right; they are dependent on the Scripture, which is THE authority.

It needs to be seen that genuine *sola Scriptura* of the Reformation sort is not quite what various of the early church fathers thought. In their view the Scriptures, including the increasingly collected and combined documents written by the apostles, eyewitnesses, and their coworkers as well as the OT, were the primary authority, but there were *other* very valuable Christian traditions that had some authority and should be used to guide the Christian life. Good examples of such noncanonical documents are the Didache and 1 Clement, and we could mention others. I don't think you can show that just because something was called a valuable Christian *graphe*, or "writing," it was Scripture, even with a lowercase *s*, despite the best arguments of Jeffrey Bingham.[1]

What we find, for instance, in the Anglican tradition of the English Reformation is a return to a view that other traditions were valuable and had some authority, but that the Scriptures, *not the church*, were the *final* authority, though not the *sole* authority. It is saying too much, then, to claim the phrase *sola Scriptura* in its most narrow sense was or is the Protestant position on the Bible.[2] Certainly it is the view of many conservative Protestants, particularly Reformed ones, and one can make the case this was the view of some German and Swiss Reformers, but they did not and do not speak for everyone in the Protestant Church—not even for all the Reformed churches.

For example, in our comparison of Lightfoot to Lewis, the former sounds much more like the Reformers on the issue of inerrancy than the latter, despite modern Evangelicals' love of Lewis. It will be well at this juncture to spend some time interacting with the recent Reformed tradition's take on this issue as expressed by several of the contributors to *Sola Scriptura! The Protestant Position on the Bible.*

This book gets off to a bad start in chapter 1 by not realizing that (1) the Catholic Church of today is not the same as the medieval church, especially since the Vatican II recognition that Protestants are fellow Christians and not heretics; (2) there was a joint statement by Catholics and Lutherans in 1999 agreeing on justification by grace through faith as an essential understanding of salvation; (3) the church all along before the Reformation, including the writers of the NT, valued traditions of various sorts in noncanonical writings[3] and believed they had some truth in them and thus some authority to speak to Christians; (4) sola Scriptura *is a phrase first used by Catholics critical of the abuses and falsehoods of the Papacy during the Middle Ages*; and (5) Vatican II produced an encyclical entitled *Dei Verbum* delineating more clearly the relationship between Scripture and other Christian tradition. There seems to be little recognition of the impact of Vatican II and such statements on Catholic life and thought since Vatican II in 1962–1965, which was more than fifty years ago.[4]

There is frankly no justification in the twenty-first century for making pronouncements like that of Robert Godfrey: "We Protestants have declared that the Roman church is a false church for adding human traditions to the Word of God."[5] Clearly, he is speaking for some very conservative Reformed Protestants but not for Protestants in general today. And then there is the bad exegesis of texts like Rev 22.18–19:

> [18] I warn everyone who hears the words of the prophecy of this scroll: If anyone adds anything to them, God will add to that person the plagues described in this scroll.

¹⁹ And if anyone takes words away from this scroll of prophecy, God will take away from that person any share in the tree of life and in the Holy City, which are described in this scroll.

Clearly, this warning is about "this scroll" and not altering the prophetic words in it. It is not about the much later fact that it turned out to be the last book in the NT canon. John of Patmos did not think he was referring to the whole Bible! Good historical contextual exegesis rules that idea out.

Godfrey goes on to clarify that what he mainly means is that the Word of God is clear enough that ordinary people can hear it, understand it, and embrace its message of salvation without depending on a particular group of church leaders, priests, and the like to interpret it for them. On this matter I doubt much of anyone could disagree. In regard to salvation the Bible is clear, and it doesn't take a scholar to interpret the truth of that idea. Fair enough, but we didn't need outdated polemics against Catholics to make a point that both Catholics and Protestants are in basic agreement on.

John Wesley, a Protestant who valued all sorts of ideas and traditions not found in Scripture, in regard to the matter of how one can be saved pronounced himself *homo unius libri*, "a man of one book," the Bible, when it comes to soteriology. This does not mean, and indeed never meant, that the Bible is perfectly clear to everyone on any topic it addresses.

Notice for example what 2 Pet 3 says about the writings of Paul (which includes the statement of 2 Tim 3.16 that Godfrey bases his conclusions on): after referring to "our dear brother Paul," he adds, "His letters contain some things that are hard to understand, which ignorant and unstable people distort, as they do the other Scriptures, to their own destruction" (2 Pet 3.15–16). The writer admits that *not everything* is perfectly clear in what Paul has written on any and every topic. While he adds that the ignorant twist the text in various ways, that is in addition to his admission that there are things that are hard to understand in Paul. And he is clear enough that he thinks Paul is writing Scripture that should be compared to other Scriptures. Again, if the issue is whether we need something in addition to the Bible today to know the truth of God *for salvation*, then the answer of almost all Christians, Catholic, Protestant, or Orthodox, should, and I would suspect would, be no.

Godfrey goes on to cite a statement from Vatican II: "It is clear, therefore, that sacred tradition, sacred Scripture, and the teaching authority of the Church, in accord with God's most wise design, are so linked and joined together that one cannot stand without the others, and that all together and each in its own way under the action of the one Holy Spirit contribute effectively to the salvation of souls."[6]

Here is a statement that Protestants can and should take issue with. These three "authorities" are not of equal standing or equally necessary to the salvation of persons. A man lost on a desert island with nothing but his Bible can be saved without the aid of tradition or the teaching authority of the Catholic Church. Protestants quite rightly say that only the Bible does and should have final authority in such matters. And it is not true that the Bible and its authority cannot stand without the aid of

Catholic tradition or the teaching office of the Catholic Church.

But it is right to wonder whether it is not high time for a Vatican III, because most of the Catholic scholars I interact with have issues with placing tradition and a particular church's teaching office on the level of equal authority with the Bible. Yes, they believe Catholic tradition and the teaching office have some necessary authority for the life of Catholic Christians, but frankly this is hardly different from Protestants who think that their pastors, their confessions of faith (like the Westminster Confession), and their scholars have a similar authority as they try and understand the Bible and all sorts of matters not directly connected to "how then shall we be saved." The Chicago Statement of Inerrancy would have had no force or effect if many Protestants didn't trust and accept the authority of those who offered that interpretation of inerrancy. While the writers of the statement might demur from such a claim, de facto it is true.

Godfrey is right that there is a critique in the NT itself of any tradition that is used to neuter or even nullify some specific teaching in the Scripture. For instance, Jesus complains about the Pharisees, "You nullify the word of God for the sake of your tradition" (Matt 15.6b). And yes, there are plenty of Catholic traditions that Protestants think are at odds with the basic teachings of the Bible itself: for example, some of the traditions about Mary, such as her perpetual virginity (and sinlessness). Most Protestants would say a careful historical contextual exegesis of the Gospels makes very likely that Mary, a devout Jewish woman living life as a Jew, not a later Catholic (with its exaltation of asceticism that came to be connected with sinlessness), had children after Jesus. This is why the brothers and sisters of Jesus are called just that—they are not called cousins in the Greek, nor stepbrothers and stepsisters. Most Protestants would likewise say that Mary was not sinless. There were things she didn't understand about her own Son, and it led to attempts to intervene in his ministry of exorcism and take him home in Mark 3.21–35 and before that to scold Jesus for being about his Father's business in Luke 2.41–52. One can say she was being a protective mother and was well-intentioned, but this sort of intervention Jesus did not need, and frankly it is at the least a sin of interference with God's will, as are many sins.

Needless to say, there is also nothing in the Bible about Mary's bodily assumption into heaven, not least because there are two different very early non-Protestant traditions about where she is buried—one involving Jerusalem and one involving Ephesus. Catholic tradition, even Catholic dogma, must past the test of the final authority, Scripture. As Godfrey goes on to point out, at various points in Catholic Church history, important scholars have disputed, and indeed denied, that the pope is the head of the church, the bishop over all the other bishops (indeed even over the patriarchs of the Eastern church).

Gregory the Great, himself a pope in Rome (540–604 A.D.), said this: "I confidently affirm that whoever calls himself *sacerdos universalis*, or desires to be so called by others is in his pride a forerunner of Antichrist."[7] What is clear from a careful study of the ante-Nicene and Nicene church fathers is that the early church did not understand the bishop of Rome or the Roman "church" itself in the way that the Roman Catholic Church came to view both popes and the Roman church in the Middle Ages. Indeed, even bishops like John Chrysostom would be very surprised to hear some of the pronouncements of the popes and the Western church in the Middle Ages. Not just Gregory the Great but others would have loudly objected to what their church had become at the expense of the final authority of the Bible, as we have already seen with some late medieval figures such as Marsilius and William of Ockham and John Wycliffe.

It is, of course, true that Catholics have often used the argument that the church formed the NT canon and there-fore the final authority lies with the church, not with the Bible itself. The historical problems with this argument are many, and here are some of the more important ones: (1) Already in the NT period Paul's letters were recognized by NT writers as Scripture like the OT Scripture. Indeed, Paul himself believed he preached and wrote the Word of God under divine inspiration, and he did not need some church leader or church council to tell him this was true. (2) The Gospels and a collection of Paul's letters were already recognized as Scripture in the second and third cen-turies A.D., long before there was agreement in the church as to which twenty-seven books made up the NT. What we see here is a gradual process of recognition by orthodox Christians of which books were God-breathed and should be preached and taught in the churches, and so it is right to talk about the church, under the guidance of the Holy

Spirit, in the fourth century *recognizing the canon*, not *deciding on and forming the canon*.[8] (3) Historically this becomes all the more obvious when three different areas of the church said these twenty-seven books and no others, including in Egypt, in Africa, and yes, with Pope Damascus in Rome, but he was by no means the first to say so in the fourth century. Notice that there was no ecumenical council or pronouncement to decide this matter; there was simply agreement in three regions of the church and that settled the matter. In fact, it took the Roman Church until the Council of Trent in 1546, in reaction to the German and Swiss Reformations, to make an official pronouncement as to what counted as canon.[9] But the issue had been settled long before then, and not just in the Western church.

Godfrey does a good job of showing how even Augustine, writing between 397 and 427 A.D., did not look to popes or councils to decide the issue of what counts as Scripture; in fact, he affirmed the discernment process in a plurality of churches.[10] Indeed, he is able to show the various disagreements within Roman Catholicism about the Bible and other matters throughout the history of that denomination, disagreements not resolved by having a pope, or a teaching office, or what came to be called the magisterium. In this regard, the history of Protestants shows we have been as bad or even worse for anathematizing each other about our beliefs, including about how we view the authority of the Bible. There is a parody of a classic hymn that sadly encapsulates things all too well when it comes to all Christians being more unified as a body of Christ:

Like a mighty turtle moves the church of God
Christians we are treading where we've always trod
not united Christians
not one body we
we will all be standing here until eternity
Backward Christian soldiers . . .

James White, in his review of what the early church fathers have to say about *sola Scriptura* (without using that precise phrase), doesn't lack for material. At the outset he cites Cyril of Jerusalem (313–386 A.D.) as saying, "In regard to the divine and holy mysteries of the faith, not the least part may be handed on without the Holy Scriptures. Do not be led astray by winning words and clever arguments. Even to me, who tell you these things, do not give ready belief, unless you receive from the Holy Scriptures the proof of the things which I announce. The salvation in which we believe is not proved from clever reasoning, but from the Holy Scriptures."[11] We have already noted words to this effect in our earlier chapters by some church fathers. White is right to emphasize such material.[12]

He is also right to take on the very dubious notion that the distinctive Catholic doctrines later made official and even dogma were part of "unwritten apostolic traditions" from the beginning. One may rightly ask how subsequent generations can fully rely upon such traditions if they were unwritten, only passed along orally. But when church fathers mention traditions not found in the NT, they are *nearly always referring to known documents*, not "unwritten traditions." Let us take, for instance, the tradition that Peter was the first pope in Rome. One of the salient points to make about the distinctive Catholic doctrines is that, as I have already shown with various of the distinctive claims of various forms of Evangelical theology, it is precisely where a Christian tradition tries to claim something distinctive that there is the least scriptural or historical support for such an idea.[13]

Frankly, there is no evidence in any of the earliest Christian documents for Peter being seen as the first pope in Rome. In fact, we don't even have early evidence for his being a bishop over Rome (see below). This is not impossible, but one would need actual early evidence to substantiate the claim. First Peter suggests his authority was over churches in what today we call Turkey, not in Rome.

J. B. Lightfoot long ago demonstrated that the notion of the succession of an *apostolic* office was dubious, and even more doubtful is the notion that Peter founded the church in Rome. On the latter point, the earliest Christian witnesses, including Paul's Letter to the Romans, make perfectly clear the church already existed in Rome long before Paul or Peter ever got there, and the evidence suggests he got there after Paul did in 60 A.D.

Lightfoot stresses, "Now I cannot find that any writers for the first two centuries and more speak of S. Peter as bishop of Rome. Indeed, their language is inconsistent with the assignment of this position to him. When Dionysius of Corinth speaks of the Apostles S. Peter and S. Paul as *jointly* planting the two Churches of Corinth and of Rome, he obviously cannot mean this; for otherwise he would point to a divided episcopate."[14] Paul was welcomed by the church in Rome when he arrived in about 60 A.D. (see Acts 28), as we assume Peter was later. As Lightfoot goes on to point out, Paul was never called bishop of Corinth or Philippi, though he founded the churches there. In fact, *neither Peter nor Paul founded the church in Rome.*

In his essay "On the Christian Ministry," Lightfoot stresses that while we can demonstrate the passing on of the apostolic *tradition* in the first and second centuries and the establishment of the episcopal office (i.e., bishops), we can't demonstrate the passing on of an *apostolic* office from Peter to others. Bishops yes, apostles no.[15] This would have been Paul's conclusion as well, because to him Apostle (with a capital *A*) meant someone who had seen and been commissioned by the risen Lord, and Paul says he was the last of these. Apostle with a small *a* simply meant a missionary commissioned by a particular church to evangelize somewhere, as we see the term used in Luke-Acts.

White goes on to rightly stress that the "traditions" to which Irenaeus refers are those found in the OT and NT, not the later Catholic traditions about Mary or the Papacy or papal infallibility.[16] Irenaeus cannot be used to back up later Catholic claims about matters Irenaeus nowhere mentions. White's argument in regard to Basil of Caesarea (329–79) is less convincing because Basil does refer to unwritten traditions followed by his church, but when he tells us what they are, they turn out *not to be what the later Catholic tradition was talking about.* They were things like facing east when praying or triune baptism like the Eastern church came to practice. White rightly points out that when there was controversy over church traditions between churches that the final authority to decide the issue needed to be not "oral tradition" but Scripture, citing Basil's instruction: "Therefore let God-inspired Scripture decide between us; and on whichever side be found doctrines in harmony with the word of God, in favor of that side will be cast the vote of truth" (*NPNF²* 8:229, Letter 189: To Eustathius the physician).

White's defense of Athanasius on the matter of the final authority of Scripture seems to be mostly on target. Athanasius, however much he may have valued extrabiblical traditions, after all did indeed see Scripture as the final authority. For instance, he says in his treatise *Against the Heathen*, "For indeed the holy and God-breathed Scripture are self-sufficient for the preaching of the truth" (in PG 25:4). Likewise, in his *Letter to the Bishops of Egypt and Libya*, he says, "But since Holy Scripture is of all things most sufficient for us, therefore recommend to those who desire to know more of these matters, to read the divine Word" (PG 25:548).

All in all, the book in which Godfrey's and White's essays appear does bring together some evidence that is helpful in the discussion of *sola Scriptura* and is to be commended for that, but it still makes some erroneous statements about the phrase and its origins and about what the current spectrum of teaching is today in the Catholic Church, as the good interaction with Joseph Fitzmyer's commentary on Romans by S. B. Ferguson demonstrates.[17] This book shows that the concept and the interpretation of the concept of *sola Scriptura* is alive and well.

What has become clear in regard to the recent history of most if not all of the so-called mainline Protestant Churches is that when a denomination defects from some major theological or ethical truth in Scripture, many Christians leave them, as in the case of the Episcopal Church, Presbyterian USA, Lutheran LCA, and now the UMC Methodists. In *all these cases*, the main presenting issue is a change of approach to issues of human sexuality and Christian marriage. This has now led to the formation of other Episcopal (Anglican), Presbyterian, Lutheran, and now Methodist churches. What this shows is that conservative Protestants of whatever stripe still care about fidelity to what they take as the ethical imperatives of Scripture, and perhaps more importantly they are still convicted that the Bible itself should be the final authority in such matters, not the shifting sands of the larger culture or the pronouncement of some bishops or clergy.

So, going forward, what is the future for the *sola Scriptura* idea? Inasmuch as the truth of Scripture will always be relevant, a source of revelation, inspiration, and changed lives, and indeed the source for evangelism and missionary work for all those who firmly believe that the world is lost and desperately needs the gospel, a gospel that makes exclusive claims that salvation is to be found in no other person than Jesus Christ, then yes—the future for the notion of *sola Scriptura* is bright because only the Bible provides the impetus and the truth content to justify such activity. The living Word of God is desperately needed in our world, and it provides the only solution to the human dilemma.

As for the term "inerrancy," different though equally devout Christians define the term differently. To the young earth enthusiast, it includes the notion that the Bible *teaches* the idea that the earth is only a few thousand years old. To others, it means that the Bible *teaches* a particular sort of Reformed theology, in particular Calvinism. To still others it means that the Bible *teaches* that the initial evidence of being a born-again Spirit-filled Christian is that one speaks in tongues, like Cornelius and his family in Acts 10. To still others it means that the Bible *teaches* adult baptism, perhaps even baptism by immersion. And I could go on. The definitions of inerrancy are like the period of the Judges, "each one doing what is right in his own eyes."

The Chicago Statement is perhaps the best good-faith effort to narrow down what inerrancy does and doesn't mean. But even then, it is not completely clear from that statement how the relationship of science and faith should be seen. As I have said repeatedly, I think that the subjects the Bible actually teaches us on are theology, ethics, history, in particular salvation history, and spiritual formation. I think that one also must make a distinction between what the Bible merely mentions or touches and what it teaches. The statement in 2 Tim 3.16 about the God-breathed nature of Scripture goes on to stress that Scripture is profitable and sufficient for teaching, rebuking, correcting, and training in particular things like righteousness, which certainly includes ethics. Notice it does not give us a long list of subjects it is teaching us about. In fact, 2 Tim 3.16 is mainly about ethics.

As the Chicago Statement's later addendums in the 1980s also make clear, hermeneutics, or the art of interpretation, is a key to this whole issue. Prose should be interpreted as prose, poetry as poetry, wisdom literature as wisdom literature, salvation history as salvation history, and so on. And one needs some clear knowledge of how ancient covenants work. Most of all, historical contextual exegesis is all important, for as I like to say, a text without a context is just a pretext for whatever one wants it to say and mean.[18]

CODA

To sum up, before the modern era the vast majority of recorded Christian views on Scripture and its authority have been very high indeed, and all of them involve a considerable view of divine inspiration and the truth content of the Scriptures themselves. Sometimes what this amounted to is seeing Scripture as the *main* authority in the church or the *final* authority in the church, but before there were severe power abuses and corruption in the Papacy, the phrase *sola Scriptura* doesn't seem to have come up, and it first appeared on the lips of Catholics, not Reformers or later Protestants. *The notion that the church or the pope, not Scripture, is the final authority in matters of faith and practice cannot be traced back to the earliest period of Christianity.* This is in part because in the apostolic era, the leaders of the movement were almost all Jews, and they all not only manifested great reverence for what we call the OT but saw themselves as *under its authority*, before and after they became followers of Christ.

As for the relationship of Scripture and other valuable traditions, a variety of views existed about this matter, but none before the German Reformation and not all of them afterward amounted to the neglecting or dismissing of other valuable Christian traditions, or failing to allow those traditions to have *some* authority for Christian life.

Sola Scriptura meant and means Scripture alone only for some Christians at and after the Reformation and into the modern era. De facto, what it normally means even in those circles is that Scripture is supposed to be the final authority on all matters of faith and practice, on things the Bible actually teaches.

At the same time, there was no patience with forgeries when they were discovered in the early church. Forgeries were not seen by Christians as a legitimate literary practice, not in the case of epistolary pseudepigrapha, or Gospels or Apocalypses falsely attributed to one of the Twelve, or much later documents reported to have been written by Constantine. This was true even in the earliest period of the Christian church.[19] This is not to say that there were no such documents. *Of course* there were, but when their character was discovered, they were prohibited from being read in church as Scripture, and, in the case of genuinely heterodox documents, church fathers like Athanasius told his monks and priests to get rid of them, which is why so many gnostic documents have been found at the ancient garbage dump at Nag Hammadi. Before Athanasius, the Muratorian Canon labels two epistles attributed to Paul as forgeries composed by the supporters of Marcion.

If we follow the lead of wise Christian interpreters of the Bible like J. B. Lightfoot, we will value the lessons we learn from whatever source we learn them from, since all truth is God's truth. We will value Christian traditions, especially early ones from before the church became both almost entirely gentile in character and sadly anti-Semitic and paradoxically at the same time pro-patriarchal and in favor of Levitical models of ministries (e.g., having priests, temples, and sacrifices, which of course excluded women from such activities).

We will also value both reason and experience. Not that any of these three (tradition, reason, or experience) should be seen as *independent* or *infallible* authorities for the Christian life or things that can *trump* what the Bible actually *teaches* on matters of theology, ethics, salvation history, and spiritual formation. If there is a red thread that we can trace throughout Christian history in regard to the Scriptures, it is that that the Scriptures should be seen as the *final* authority for faith and practice, as the litmus test for all other authority claims by tradition, reason, or experience. If church history teaches us anything about how and when the church has gone wrong, it is when the Scriptures were *not* viewed or lived as the *final* authority for the Christian church and its members. The telltale sign of theology gone wrong is when it is not well-grounded in or supported by the ultimate authority—Holy Scripture. May God give us discernment in all these matters in these turbulent and even chaotic times.

Appendix

As It Turns Out—The Bible Is Not Pro-slavery

Over the course of some forty years of teaching the Bible, I have become increasingly weary of the misreading of the slave passages in both the OT and the NT. This frustration was only exacerbated when the Museum of the Bible had a special exhibit a couple of years ago of *The Slaves' Bible*, a Bible produced by slaveholders in the United Kingdom for the colonies, where slavery was the very means by which rice and cotton plantations (and other sorts as well) operated to produce great wealth for plantation owners. This Bible cut out all scriptural passages that might suggest that slavery was not God's design for Africans in relationship to the white race. But if the Bible was such an advocate of slavery, why would about 25% of its relevant verses need to be deleted? Why would a passage like Gal 3.28 need to be left out altogether? Let me say at the outset that I understand that the Bible was often used as tool to advocate slavery. This was true in my native region of the South in the United States. And here is where I quote a famous Latin dictum—"Abusus non tollit usum." The abuse of a text does not rule out its proper use. Misinterpretation of the slave passages has been rampant throughout the last 2,000 years, and in an ironic twist, that same misinterpretation today is used to dismiss the Bible's authority when it comes to ethical matters, including not only slavery but also other hot button issues such as sexual orientation and same-sex sexual activity. What's wrong with this picture? Much indeed.

Let me start with a theological point too often overlooked entirely in such discussions. We live in a fallen world, a world full of sin and self-centered behaviors of all sorts. And a fallen human being has an infinite capacity to justify his self-serving behavior and preferences. This fallenness has led not only to the enslaving of some human beings by others, but also to patriarchy. It is no accident that while the beginning of the Bible tells us that "male and female," God created them equally in his own image, that after the "original sin" story we learn that part of the curse on humanity involves "your [a wife's] desire will be for your husband and he will lord it over you." This is not the creation order design, this is the curse that falls upon humans because they chose sin over obeying God's commandment. And it is no accident either that after that original sin we hear for the first time about violence—about brother killing brother, and almost as quickly about patriarchy lived out and then slavery as well. Both of the latter involve the desire and will of some human beings, particularly males, to dominate other human beings. Slavery of course in the Bible was not primarily race based. Indeed, in the Greco-Roman world of the Roman Empire it was not based on the color of one's skin at all. It was the result of who conquered whom and thereafter who enslaved whom. So unlike in the antebellum

South in the United States, in Paul's world you had slaves who had previously been elite members of society, well-educated persons, teachers, philosophers, businesspersons, skilled artisans—and I could go on. Now I point this out because it is a fundamental mistake to read the Bible in the light of modern concerns about racism, and in particular racism on the basis of skin color as well as place of origin. Skin color was not in the main the basis of racism or slavery in antiquity. The Bible needs to be read in the light of its own context, not the context of the recent past in Europe and America (and elsewhere).

Certainly one of the dominant images and passages in the Bible when it comes to the issue of slavery is the storyline in Exodus about the enslaving of the Hebrews, and then their liberation through the efforts of Moses and others. And note that Moses was a reluctant liberator. It was God Almighty who sent Moses back to Egypt with the command to free his chosen people, and Moses was ordered—yes, ordered—to confront Pharaoh (probably Ramses II) and to tell him to "let my people go." This whole storyline should have made clear God's view of this matter of slavery, and one has to bear in mind that the Bible is not the story of everyone, everywhere. It is rather the story of the origins and salvation history of God's people, which nonetheless has implications for all other peoples as well.

Slavery in the fallen world of the ANE and in the Greco-Roman world was in large measure the basis of the economy, which made sure that wealth was in the hands of the few, and poverty was the byword of the many, especially of the slaves. In yet another twist of history, in some cases domestic slaves did much better than poor free persons, because they had food, shelter, and clothing provided, which resulted in odd epitaphs like "being a slave was never a burden or a bad thing for me." And yet of course slaves, under law, were just chattel, just property to be bought and sold, and by and large they had no legal rights at all. So when we read the slave passages in the Bible, and particularly in the NT, we need to realize that slavery was a huge long-settled institution in the ANE, and also in the Greco-Roman world. There would likely have been no seven wonders of the world, no pyramids, no temple of Artemis, no mining, no adequate agricultural economy without slavery in that world, and the secular laws simply encoded and supported that institution. But what about the Bible?

In the OT we have not only the story of the Exodus, but we have the law of Jubilee, both of which show the larger divine design that does not approve of humans enslaving other humans, and seeks to counter these domination systems. And it will be remembered that when Jesus preached his inaugural sermon in Nazareth, according to Luke 4 he cited Isaiah, which in part says he came to set the captives free, and this was not merely about being free from illness or demon possession. Jesus came to set the eschatological year of Jubilee in motion, which is why we actually have people like Paul saying after the fact "but in Christ there is neither slave nor free" (Gal 3.28 and compare the parallels). But what was someone like Paul to do with the overwhelming slave situation in his day? One estimate says that up to a third or even a half of the population of a city like Rome were slaves, and Christianity was a tiny minority religion, and there was no democracy, only autocracy. How and where could Paul advocate change?

So the strategy to live out the social implications of Gal 3.28 had to involve working for change in the relationships within the Christian household. It could not be accomplished elsewhere at the outset of the Christian movement. And Paul was practical enough to start with his converts where they were, which is to say, some of the more elite ones already had domestic slaves. So Paul chose to put the leaven of the gospel of equality and humanity into the Christian household and let that change the domination patterns from within that social context.

As I have pointed out in my commentary *Philemon, Colossians, and Ephesians* (Eerdmans, 2007), what we see is a progressive working for change. Colossians provides us with first-order moral discourse, what Paul would say as an opening salvo to a group he did not personally convert (but which seems to have been converted by one of his coworkers, perhaps Tychicus); then in Ephesians we have a circular letter written to some he had converted and some others as well, providing second-order moral discourse; then the conversation continues, and finally in Philemon we have third-order moral discourse—what Paul could and would say to someone who had slaves and someone he had personally converted, namely Philemon manumit Onesimus, who is "no longer a slave but rather a brother in Christ." Here Paul boldly tells Philemon that if someone is in Christ, there should be no slave or free. And we know that early Christians in the second century and thereafter regularly would seek to buy slaves out of slavery, trying to implement

the Pauline mandate, though it was not consistently imple-
mented. But we need to note, however, the ways Paul was
changing the status quo.

Firstly, unlike Greco-Roman household codes, which
tended to be just advice for the head of the household (the
husband, the male parent, the master), Paul by contrast
treats wives, children, and slaves as moral agents capable of
making moral decisions. He addresses them directly. And
the general drift of the threefold exhortations to the head
of the household is that Paul is changing the game, want-
ing the head of the household NOT to follow the advice of
Plutarch and others—namely, subordinate your wife, children, and slaves, and keep them all in line. In fact he gives
three times as many imperatives to the male head of the
household than to the other family members. The Colossian
household code in the first place ameliorates the approach
of the master/husband/father, ruling out harsh behavior
and discouraging language, even brutal treatment, bearing
in mind that masters had previously been told they could
beat or even kill their slaves as need be without legal con-
sequences. But let us focus on Col 4.1 for a minute. As Dr.
Murray Vasser has shown in his doctoral dissertation here at
Asbury, the Greek word ἰσότης definitely means equality. It
reads "Masters, give what is righteous and equality to your
slaves, knowing that you also have a master in heaven." Now
this is definitely countercultural. Not Plutarch, not Seneca,
not Aristotle, not Plato, not anyone was advocating that
slaves and masters shared some sort of equality, never mind
ontological equality. But this is exactly what Paul is saying.
He believes we are all created in God's image. He warns the

master that *he* has a master, namely God, and he'd better watch his behavior. And Paul has already told the slave, let your service to your human master be as service actually to the Lord. Do it as if you were just the Lord's servant and not part of a fallen human institution.

If we move on to Ephesians, Paul gets even bolder. Not only do we have the commandment in Eph 5.21 that says "submit to one another out of reverence for Christ" and involves ALL members of the household—husbands, wives, children, and slaves, who were all part of household worship in regular practice. Paul then goes on to add more. He expands the advice in Colossians in important ways. . . . Note the following. Paul says to the slaves in Eph 6:

> [7] "Serve wholeheartedly, as if you were serving the Lord, not people, [8] because you know that the Lord will reward each one for whatever good they do, whether they are slave or free.
> [9] And masters, treat your slaves in the same way. Do not threaten them, since you know that he who is both their Master and yours is in heaven, and there is no favoritism with him." (NIV)

Paul had already mentioned that God doesn't judge master or slave with partiality. But here he adds, masters, do the same thing as your slaves are doing—namely, masters serve your slaves as they serve you, bearing in mind God is your master as well as theirs. This is very clearly second-order moral discourse, which goes beyond the instructions in Colossians. And then of course there is Philemon. Now all this while, Paul has been working toward Gal 3.28, gradually implementing change in the Christian household to both domination systems—patriarchy and slavery. He is wise enough to implement change in this way because he knows he must start with his audience where they are and, through persuasion and imperatives, implement change to these longstanding institutions. But with Philemon, the man who humanly speaking owes Paul his very spiritual life as a Christian, he can be direct—to Philemon he simply says, manumit Onesimus and send him back to me. Now if indeed Onesimus was a runaway slave, and particularly if he had owed the master anything, besides just his regular work, Paul offered to repay Philemon, but does so tongue in cheek: "Oh did I mention that you, Philemon, owe me your very everlasting life!" This is not subtle. By law, Philemon had every right to beat his returning slave or even "terminate" him. Instead, here Onesimus stands in the household meeting with the letter to Philemon in hand, which is read out before the whole house church. This puts pressure on Philemon not only to be forgiving and treat Onesimus well but to set him free!! (and on this see my friend Tom Wright's discussion about Philemon in his *Paul and the Faithfulness of God*).

Now the upshot of all this is that one cannot fairly treat what the Bible says about slavery as an excuse to say, "Well, the Bible advocates slavery, and therefore we have a right to ignore various of its other ethical teachings, since we moderns now know better." Of course the irony is that those who say these things think they are being so progressive, and in touch with the times in the West. But in fact, what is happening is they are using such dismissal of the Bible's ethical teachings and mandates as an excuse to be an advocate for a sort of ethic, including a sexual ethic that has much more in common with first-century pagan sexual ethics than with biblical teaching. It reminds me of that great scene in Shakespeare's Henry plays, where Prince Hal has been out carousing all night with Falstaff while the king stays up late, upset with this behavior; when the two finally arrive home, the king says in effect, "you think you are so *au courant*, but in fact you are just committing the oldest kinds of sins in the newest kinds of ways." I'm afraid that is the state of play in much of American culture today. As it turns out, the earliest Christians were more ethical than we are. Like many early Jews, they even abhorred abortion and rescued children who had been exposed and left out to die, which often happened particularly to unwanted baby girls. But that's a story for another day.

Notes

1 THE PEOPLE OF THE BOOK

1 *M. Scil.* 12 (i.e., *Martyrum Scillitanorum acta*) from about 180 A.D.

2 In what follows I am indebted to C. T. R. Hayward, "Scripture in the Jerusalem Temple," in *The New Cambridge History of the Bible*, vol. 1, *From the Beginnings to 600*, ed. J. C. Paget and J. Schaper (Cambridge: Cambridge University Press, 2013), 321ff.

3 Contra Lee MacDonald, *The Biblical Canon: Its Origin, Transmission, and Authority*, 2nd ed. (Grand Rapids: Baker, 2006). The reference to 1 Enoch in Jude is not an exception to this rule, as Jude is not citing that text as Scripture but rather as a true word from a prophet, which would be no different, for example, from citing Balaam offering a true or inspired word from the biblical God. I am not here primarily concerned about various views of sacred texts prior to the Second Temple period. What is true, however, even during the Second Temple period, is that Samaritans, and apparently some Sadducees, did not agree with the majority view represented by Josephus and also at Qumran, as they limited Holy Writ only to the Pentateuch.

4   Hayward, "Scripture in the Jerusalem Temple," 342.

5   See the Wikipedia article, which is excellent (https://
     en.wikipedia.org/wiki/Tertullian, last edited on May 7,
     2023), and the comment there: "For Tertullian scripture
     was authoritative, he used scripture as the primary source
     in almost every chapter of his every work, and very rarely
     anything else. He seems to prioritize the authority of scrip-
     ture above anything else." Tertullian was followed in talking
     about a "new testament" by Clement of Alexandria, who
     uses the phrase regularly and in the sense later Christians
     would use it; see H. van Campenhausen, *The Formation of the
     Christian Bible* (Philadelphia: Fortress, 1972), 293ff.

6   See the helpful discussion by Margaret M. Mitchell, "The
     Emergence of the Written Record," in *The Cambridge His-
     tory of Christianity*, vol. 1, *Origins to Constantine*, ed. Margaret
     M. Mitchell and Frances M. Young (Cambridge: Cambridge
     University Press, 2006), 177–94.

7   Mitchell, "Emergence of the Written Record," 178.

8   Found in P. M. Blowers, *The Bible in Greek Christian Antiq-
     uity* (Notre Dame, Ind.: University of Notre Dame Press,
     1997), 15–29.

9   Paul Lamarche, "The Septuagint: The Bible of the Earliest
     Christians," in Blowers, *Bible in Greek Christian Antiquity*, 19.

10   But there is some. See, e.g., J. Ross Wagner, *Herald of the
     Good News: Isaiah and Paul in Concert in the Letter to the
     Romans* (Leiden: Brill, 2000), and more recently his *Reading
     the Sealed Book: Old Greek Isaiah and the Problem of Septuagint
     Hermeneutics* (Tübingen: Mohr Siebeck, 2013).

11   Theodotion, a Hellenistic Jew, in about 150 A.D. did his
     own translation of the Hebrew text into Greek, or possibly
     revised the LXX where needed. In any case, his version of
     the Greek OT became popular with Christians in the sec-
     ond century and seems to have been used by Justin Martyr
     and the author of the Shepherd of Hermas. His version of

Daniel was especially popular in such Christian circles. The problem is, it appears several writers of the NT (e.g., the author of Hebrews) and the author of 1 Clement seem to follow his Greek version—*which did not exist yet.* Possibly, Theodotion was drawing on other independent early Greek translations of the OT.

12 Lamarche, "Septuagint," 23, 29.

13 See the balanced discussion by M. Hengel, *The Septuagint as Christian Scripture* (Grand Rapids: Baker Academic, 2004). Even before that study, my old mentor C. K. Barrett had written a seminal article about how "Gospel and Apostle" collections of Gospels and of Paul's letters were already viewed as Christian Scripture no later than the early second century. The proof of this can be seen in how Polycarp used previous early Christian documents (on which see below). C. K. Barrett, "The First New Testament," *Novum Testamentum* 38 (1996): 94–104.

14 And there was danger when the Greco-Roman world saw these Christians as not simply some sect of Judaism. To be branded a *superstitio* meant Christians could be subject to persecution and prosecution not only under Roman law but also under some Greek law. Paul's hearing before the Areopagus in Athens in Acts 17 is precisely because he was rightly perceived to be touting a foreign religion not sanctioned by the Athenian authorities, not merely a new philosophy.

15 Notice that the reference to "the reader" (ὁ ἀναγινώσκων) in Rev 1.3–4 is distinguished from "the hearer." This is because "the reader" is the lector or literate person who read the document out loud to others and had to know in advance how to separate the endless stream of Greek letters into words, phrases, and sentences so the document made sense to the church audiences listening.

16 On this, see now Ben Witherington III and Jason A. Myers, *New Testament Rhetoric*, 2nd exp. ed. (Eugene, Ore.: Cascade, 2022).

17 Χριστιανούς, or "partisans of Christ" (Acts 11.26), is a term used by outsiders who recognized the evangelistic character of Christ followers, and is not a self-chosen title. See now Paul Trebilco, *Outsider Designations and Boundary Construction in the New Testament* (Cambridge: Cambridge University Press, 2021).

18 See the helpful review of Plutarch's voluminous writings about ancient religion at https://www.encyclopedia.com/people/history/historians-ancient-biographies/plutarch. Plutarch never mentions Christianity, nor does he say much about Judaism, but he was very well informed about polytheistic religions going all the way back to Plato's time. He himself was a priest at Delphi and believed in oracles. He also bemoaned that in his day many people had stopped believing the gods were real gods. He seems to have some issues with the emperor cult as well, particularly with Nero and later Domitian. See his *Moralia*, especially his tract on superstition, and "Atheism," paras. 11–12.

19 A. D. Nock, *Conversion* (Baltimore: Johns Hopkins University Press, 1998). The original publication of this highly influential work was in 1933.

20 Apuleius (124–170 A.D.) lived when Christianity was definitely on the rise in numerous places in the empire, including where he lived. His is the oldest Latin novel extant.

21 See Rodney Stark, *The Rise of Christianity* (Princeton: Princeton University Press, 1996).

22 See especially the seminal essays by E. A. Judge found in a volume edited by another of my old mentors, David Scholer—E. A. Judge, *Social Distinctives of the Christians in the First Century*, ed. David Scholer (Grand Rapids: Baker Academic, 2007).

23 Harry Gamble, "Marcion and the Canon," in Mitchell and Young, *Cambridge History of Christianity*, 1:195–213, here 211.

24 Luke Wilson, "How Polycarp (and Others) Show the Early Use of the New Testament," The Sacred Faith, updated November 21, 2021, https://www.thatancientfaith .uk/home/perma/1637485200/article/polycarp-show-the -early-use-of-the-new-testament.html.

25 On which, see Ben Witherington III, *John's Wisdom* (Louis-ville: Westminster John Knox, 1995).

26 My friend Prof. Warren Smith noted about Serapion, "That the church at Rhossus had to ask about the Gospel of Peter and that Serapion had not heard of the Gospel of Peter when the church at Rhossus initially asked him about its authority indicates that that the canon was not set, i.e., they are open to the possibility that there are other legitimate gospels to the four we recognize. That Serapion was theoretically receptive to the Gospel of Peter on the grounds of apostolicity indi-cates, however, that the concern for a link to the apostles, as was seen in Ignatius (who claimed that the gospels of Jesus were the 'original documents') and Irenaeus, treated them not only as authoritative for the sake of right doctrine but also as having greater authority than the OT. That Serapion rejected the Gospel of Peter on the grounds that it did not conform to the apostolic teachings—presumably contained in the other Gospels and the oral tradition—indicates that those texts together with the oral tradition serve as the litmus test for true apostolicity" (private correspondence).

27 See the discussion and critique of the late date in Ben With-erington III, *What's in the Word* (Waco: Baylor University Press, 2009). It seems very clear that the clumsy seventh-century Latin ms. is an example of an attempt to translate the earlier Greek document.

28 See Geoffrey Mark Hahneman, *The Muratorian Fragment and the Development of the Canon* (Oxford: Clarendon, 1992). For the original document in Latin, see Muratori, *Antiquitates Italicae Medii Aevi* (Milan, 1740), 3:809–80.

29 The still-standard reference work dealing with these matters is my old teacher Bruce Metzger's *The Canon of the New Testament: Its Origin, Development, and Significance* (Oxford: Clarendon, 1997), 191–201, 305–307. This is to be preferred to the work of his former doctoral student, Bart Ehrman, *Lost Christianities: The Battle for Scripture and the Faiths We Never Knew* (Oxford: Oxford University Press, 2003), which is full of questionable judgments about these matters.

30 I have changed the word "made" in the original to "composed" to avoid confusion.

31 "Tertullian," Wikipedia, accessed December 24, 2022, https://en.wikipedia.org/wiki/Tertullian. On the vexed question of Tertullian and his use of Paul's letters, see Todd D. Still and David E. Wilhite, eds., *Tertullian and Paul* (New York: Bloomsbury, 2013).

32 Jeffrey Bingham, "Senses of Scripture in the Second Century: Irenaeus, Scripture, and Noncanonical Christian Texts," *Journal of Religion* 97, no. 1 (2017), accessed December 24, 2022, https://www.journals.uchicago.edu/doi/10.1086/688994.

33 Bingham, "Senses of Scripture," 27, 30, 32.

34 Norman Geisler, "Irenaeus on Scripture and Tradition," 2014, https://normangeisler.com/irenaeus-tradition-scripture/.

35 See the discussion of M. Jourjon, "Irenaeus's Reading of the Bible," in Blowers, *Bible in Greek Christian Antiquity*, 105–11, here 108.

36 Here Jourjon is paraphrasing and then quoting Irenaeus. "Irenaeus's Reading," 109.

37 D. Minns, "Truth and Tradition: Irenaeus," in Mitchell and Young, *Cambridge History of Christianity*, 1:261–73, here 268.

38 Ronald Heine, "Reading the Bible with Origen," in Blowers, *Bible in Greek Christian Antiquity*, 132.

39 And see the discussion by Heine, "Reading the Bible," 132–37.

40 On which, see Ben Witherington III, "Did the Canon Misfire?" chap. 6 in *The Living Word of God* (Waco: Baylor University Press, 2020), 113–35.

41 See the bibliography for complete citation details of the volumes containing these quotes.

42 Margaret M. Mitchell, *The Heavenly Trumpet* (Louisville: Westminster John Knox, 2002), 296.

43 Here I am not referring to Origen's allegorical interpretation because we see this already in Clement of Alexandria, and before that in Philo's interpretation of the OT. I am referring to the willingness to say that some biblical texts involved some historical inaccuracies.

44 Jean-Noël Guinot, "Theodoret of Cyrus: Bishop and Exegete," in Blowers, *Bible in Greek Christian Antiquity*, 163–93, here 164–65.

2 THE ORIGINS OF *SOLA SCRIPTURA*

1 Philip Schaff, *History of the Christian Church*, vol. 6, *The Middle Ages, A.D. 1294–1517* (New York: Scribner's, 1910; repr., Grand Rapids: Eerdmans, 1980), 76, citing Marsiglius, *Interpretatio ex communi concilio fidelium facta, etc.*, 3.1.

2 Sinaiticus in fact is in variable condition depending on which part we are referring to. It seems to have included all the OT, as did the LXX. What has survived today is about half of the Greek Old Testament, along with a complete New Testament, the entire deuterocanonical books, plus the Epistle of Barnabas and portions of the Shepherd of Hermas. The question is, should this be seen as a canon list prior to 367 A.D. or just a collection of approved Christian documents?

3 Wycliffe had been constantly harassed after various of his pronouncements and would not be quiet. He was banished from his place at Oxford and relegated to a parish in Lutterworth, and on December 28, 1384, he had a stroke while saying Mass, a Mass in which he did not believe transubstantiation was involved. Only shortly thereafter in 1401, Parliament passed an anti-Wycliffe statute that extended the persecution to Wycliffe's remaining followers. His tracts and books were banned. This foreshadowed what was to happen to William Tyndale, who was literally martyred.

4 This is well chronicled in the older treatments in Schaff's *History of the Christian Church*, vol. 6, which covers the period 1294–1517, which is to say from the time of Pope Boniface VIII to Martin Luther.

5 See his treatise entitled *Interpretatio ex communi concilio fidelium facta, etc.*, 3.1. See Philip Schaff, *The Creeds of Christendom* (Grand Rapids: Baker, 1998), 1:61–69. Marsilius was not the only one to make such a suggestion. As the helpful Wikipedia article on *sola Scriptura* adds, "Johann Ruchrat von Wesel . . . and Johannes von Goch also foreshadowed the Protestant view of *sola scriptura*: they viewed the scripture as being the only infallible authority and denied the authority of the pope or the church as infallible" (https://en.wikipedia.org/wiki/ Sola_scriptura, last edited May 15, 2023).

6 Schaff, *History of the Christian Church*, 6:73. The full text can be seen online at https://ccel.org/ccel/schaff/hcc6/hcc6.iii.ii .vii.html, under heading 8, n. 141.

7 As noted, it was Lorenzo Valla a century later who was to show that the Donation of Constantine was a forgery. William of Ockham himself does not argue for this. He simply thinks it was a bad decision by a ruler. Marsilius also rejected the Donation, but he also doesn't appear to argue it was a forgery.

8   Schaff, *History of the Christian Church*, 6:71. Cf. https://ccel
    .org/ccel/schaff/hcc6/hcc6.iii.ii.vii.html, first two paras.
    under heading 8.

9   This is a very nice translation of the Middle English by Ruth M.
    Stauffer, excerpted from the Christian History Institute web-
    site: https://christianhistoryinstitute.org/magazine/article/
    chaucers-parson.

10 As J. B. Lightfoot shows, Wycliffe is not alone in this exege-
    sis of that crucial text. On which see below, pp. 34–39.

11 Schaff, *History of the Christian Church*, 6:338. Schaff spends a
    great deal of time, quite rightly, on Wycliffe. On Wycliffe's
    view on the Scriptures, see 338–49.

12 Schaff, *History of the Christian Church*, 6:346.

13 Some portions of what follows here and in the next chapter
    are excerpted from my *JETS* lecture, "Sola Scriptura and the
    Reformation," *Journal of the Evangelical Theological Society* 60,
    no. 4 (2017): 817–28. I should also say at the outset that I
    am deeply indebted to the various experts who wrote arti-
    cles for *The New Cambridge History of the Bible*, vol. 3, *From
    1450–1750*, ed. Euan Cameron (Cambridge: Cambridge Uni-
    versity Press, 2016), without whom this chapter would have
    been far less substantive and on target; see especially the
    essays by Alastair Hamilton, Jill Kraye, and Richard Rex.

14 Roger Bacon, *Opus majus*, 1:87, 110.

15 Unfortunately, Bede based his opinion on the calcula-
    tions of a monk named Dionysius Exiguus, who lived from
    about 470–544. This calculation placed the birth of Christ
    after the time of the death of Herod the Great, which the
    birth narratives in Matthew, especially, rule out. Herod
    died somewhere between 6 and 2 B.C. See my "The Turn
    of the Christian Era: The Tale of Dionysius Exeguus," *Bib-
    lical Archaeology Review* 43, no. 6 (2017): 26, https://www
    .baslibrary.org/biblical-archaeology-review/43/6/8.

16 While Orthodoxy maintained a continual focus on the Greek of the NT, it also privileged the Greek OT, the LXX, and to this day Orthodox divines are resistant to the principle that translations of the OT should be based on the original Hebrew text. For them, the whole Bible is in Greek, and the Greek OT is authoritative and canonical. Protestantism not only reacted to the Latin Vulgate; its principle of original language as a basis for translation put it into conflict with Orthodoxy as well, though on a lesser scale. I remember having arguments in the early 1980s with a student of mine who was an Orthodox monk, in regard to what to make of Isa 7:14, which of course in the LXX has *parthenos*, whereas the Hebrew uses a broader and less technical term. For him, the LXX settled the matter.

17 Battista Guarini, "A Program of Teaching and Learning," in *Humanist Educational Treatises*, ed. and trans. Craig W. Kallendorf (Cambridge, Mass.: Harvard University Press, 2002), 260–309, here 296–97.

18 Jill Kraye, "The Revival of Greek Studies in the West," in Cameron, *New Cambridge History*, 3:37–60, here 56.

19 Lorenzo Valla, *Collatio Novi Testamenti*, ed. A. Perosa (Florence: Sansoni, 1970), 8.

20 Lorenzo Valla, *Opera Omnia*, ed. E. Garin, 2 vols. (Turin: Bottega d'Erasmo, 1962), 1:803–95 for his NT annotations. Here 865.

21 Kraye, "Revival of Greek Studies," 3:58.

3   THE GERMAN AND SWISS REFORMATION

1   Martin Luther, *Luther's Works*, vol. 32, *Career of the Reformer, Part II*, ed. George W. Forell (Philadelphia: Muhlenberg Press, 1958), 112.

2   This is an actual aphorism coined in the 1520s.

3   Richard Rex, "Humanist Bible Controversies," in *The New Cambridge History of the Bible*, vol. 3, *From 1450–1750*, ed. Euan Cameron (Cambridge: Cambridge University Press, 2016), 61–81, here 64.

4 Rex, "Humanist Bible Controversies," in Cameron, *New Cambridge History*, 3:67.

5 Rex, "Humanist Bible Controversies," in Cameron, *New Cambridge History*, 3:81.

6 There is an excellent book by Andrew Pettegree entitled *Brand Luther: 1517, Printing and the Making of the Reformation* (New York: Penguin, 2005). In it, he stresses that the rise of the printing press and Luther's clear-sighted exploitation of it to publish not only his tracts and theses and commentaries but also especially his translation of the Bible were crucial factors in producing the Protestant Reformation.

7 I am aware there were some minor modifications to the Vulgate made before the time of Luther, and Luther's German translation had some precursors. However, the precursors had little or no effect on the general public in the way Luther's translation did, and the minor modifications to the Vulgate by Valla and others were just that—Erasmus kept finding more mistakes when he did his Greek NT.

8 Philip Schaff, "Luther's Translation of the Bible," in *History of the Christian Church*, vol. 7 (New York: Charles Scribner's Sons, 1910), 340–54, here 341 (emphasis added).

9 The Catholics were comparatively slow off the mark when it came to publishing an English version authorized by Rome. The first was the 1582 *Rhemes New Testament*. By then Tyndale and others had long since made their mark on the English language and English religious life.

10 See Alister McGrath, *In the Beginning: The Story of the King James Bible* (New York: Doubleday, 2001).

4   THE ENGLISH REFORMATION AND JOHN WESLEY

1 In City Road Chapel on either side of the pulpit was posted the love commandment from Leviticus and the Apostle's Creed.

2   Ken Baker, "The Puritans and the Bible," November 16, 2007, https://kenbaker.wordpress.com/2007/11/16/the-puritans-and -the-bible/. I have followed his lead in the previous paragraphs.

3   Though we can already see clear traces of this approach in some of the church fathers, for example, in Chrysostom.

4   See the citation and discussion in Michael Christensen, *C. S. Lewis on Scripture* (Nashville: Abingdon, 1979), 85.

5   William Perkins, *The Art of Prophesying* (London, 1592), included in *The Work of William Perkins*, intro. and ed. Ian Breward, 3 vols., The Courtenay Library of Reformation Classics (Sutton Berkshire: Courtenay Press, 1970), 3:338.

6   Note the remark of Wycliffe about conscience in the previous chapter.

7   By "law of Christ" Paul seems to mean (1) those portions of the old covenant reaffirmed by Christ, and in some cases intensified; (2) the new teachings of Christ not found in the OT, and in some cases annulling OT teaching; and (3) the apostolic teaching derived from and amplifying on the teachings of Christ (see, e.g., Rom 12–13).

8   See the discussion in Alister McGrath, *In the Beginning: The Story of the King James Bible* (New York: Doubleday, 2001); and my *The Living Word of God* (Waco: Baylor University Press, 2020), 127–35.

9   Which is quite different from the claim of various Greek Orthodox that the LXX is the Christian OT that has final authority and that its translators were inspired in the translating. This is rather like the conservative Protestant KJV-only folks who want to claim that the KJV translation is inspired presumably because its translators were inspired. One wonders whether they considered that various of those translators in the seventeenth century were Catholics. All versions of the KJV before 1666 included the OT Apocrypha, though it was made clear those books were of secondary authority.

10   Here is not the place to rehearse the complicated history of the rise of textual criticism of ancient manuscripts, including the Bible. For an excellent review of the attempts

to get back to the original source texts written by the original writers, see E. J. Epp's "Critical Editions of the New Testament, and the Development of Text-Critical Methods: From Erasmus to Griesbach (1516–1807)," in *The New Cambridge History of the Bible*, vol. 3, *From 1450–1750*, ed. Euan Cameron (Cambridge: Cambridge University Press, 2016), 110–37.

11 See the list in Craig L. Adams, "What John Wesley Actually Said about the Bible," 2012, http://www.cragladams.com/archive/files/john-wesley-on-the-bible.html, who in turn is summarizing Maddox.

12 Randy Maddox, "The Rule of Christian Faith, Practice, and Hope: John Wesley on the Bible," *Methodist Review* 3 (2011): 1–35, https://methodistreview.org/index.php/mr/article/view/45/68.

13 In fact, as Maddox goes on to stress, "In 1756 John Wesley published a digest of an anti-Catholic Catechism by John Williams which included an insistence that the apocryphal books were not part of 'canonical scriptures.' When he published a further redaction of this work in 1779, Wesley sharpened the point in his own words: 'We cannot but reject them. We dare not receive them as part of the Holy Scriptures.'" See also Randy Maddox, *Rethinking Wesley's Theology for Contemporary Methodism* (Nashville: Kingswood Books, 1998).

14 Wesley, as a teacher of Greek at Oxford, had four different Greek New Testaments, including Bengel's, which corrected the Textus Receptus at various points. This is of importance because the KJV committee relied on the Textus Receptus as its Greek text for translation, which clearly was not a perfect version of the Greek NT. Randy Maddox suggests this is why Wesley relied on several different translations in his teaching and preaching. See also the next note.

15 John Wesley to William Law, January 6, 1756, included in *The Letters of John Wesley*, ed. John Telford, 8 vols. (London: Epworth, 1960), 3:345.

16 See the journal entry for July 24, 1776, in John Wesley, *The Works of John Wesley*, vol. 23, *Journal and Diaries VI (1776-86)*, ed. W. Reginald Ward and Richard P. Heitzenrater (Abingdon: Nashville, 1995), 25; and the letter to the *Bristol Gazette* of September 12, 1776.

17 Maddox, "Rule of Christian Faith," 11–12.

18 See also Hope V. Dornfeld, "A Man of One Book: John Wesley's Theology of Scripture," *Diligence: Journal of the Liberty University Online Religion Capstone in Research and Scholarship* 3 (2019), article 2, https://digitalcommons.liberty.edu/djrc/vol3/iss1/2; Scott Jones, *John Wesley's Conception and Use of Scripture* (Nashville: Kingswood Books, 1995); William J. Abraham, "The Future of Scripture: In Search of a Theology of Scripture," *Wesleyan Theological Journal* 46, no. 2 (2011): 13. This comes from Rem B. Edwards, "John Wesley's Non-literal Literalism and Hermeneutics of Love," *Wesleyan Theological Journal* 51, no. 2 (2016): 26–40, https://philarchive.org/archive/EDWQWN.

19 William J. Abraham, *The Bible: Beyond the Impasse* (Dallas: Highland Loch Press, 2012).

20 In regard to tradition, Wesley accepted the Thirty-Nine Articles of the Anglican faith. He had some issues, however, with the Calvinism of the Westminster Confession on biblical grounds.

21 Jones, *John Wesley's Conception and Use of Scripture*, 216.

22 My colleague Bill Arnold rightly reminds me that sometimes the binary true/false approach does not apply to various biblical texts. He adds, "Much of the Bible is expressing emotion, exhortation, or praise. These are not truth claims that can be said to involve error or non-error, and it is wrong to impose that either/or on such texts."

23 Randy Maddox ("Rule of Christian Faith") once pondered whether Wesleyans had thought seriously enough about the implications of Arminian theology for the idea of inerrancy, namely that if the writers of the Bible had freedom of choice

about what they wrote, wouldn't they likely make some mistakes or not hear the divine revelation clearly enough? The problem with this is at least threefold: (1) A mechanical dictation theory of inspiration is not necessary to explain an accurate accounting of a revelatory experience. As Luke 1:1–4 suggests, Luke did not sit in a chair and listen to the whisperings of the Holy Spirit and then write things down; he did research and consulted eyewitnesses and others. This can be said to require divine guidance and divine providence, but it does not require divine predetermination or mechanical dictation. (2) Even without divine inspiration, people who are paying close attention can often hear something or see and learn something and repeat what they have heard accurately. (3) Second Peter 1:20–21 is pretty clear about inspired writers being carried along by the Spirit without their own style, vocabulary, etc., being overridden. Those verses say, "Above all, you must understand that no prophecy of Scripture came about by the prophet's own interpretation of things. For prophecy never had its origin in the human will, but prophets, though human, spoke from God as they were carried along by the Holy Spirit."

5 THE RISE OF MODERN SCIENCE AND THE CONSERVATIVE CHRISTIAN RESPONSE

1   Typically, ANE genealogies of kings left the skeletons in the closet, never mentioning them.

2   This is taken from Lightfoot's obituary, written by his friend and colleague, and his successor as bishop of Durham, B. F. Westcott, and it can be found in the volume I transcribed and Todd Still and I edited (assisted by Jeanette M. Hagen) of Lightfoot's notes on Acts: *The Acts of the Apostles: A Newly Discovered Commentary* (Downers Grove, Ill.: IVP, 2014), 378–79 (emphasis added). See also G. R. Treloar, *Lightfoot the Historian* (Tübingen: Mohr Siebeck, 1998).

3   J. B. Lightfoot, *The Epistles of 2 Corinthians and 1 Peter: Newly Discovered Commentaries*, ed. Ben Witherington III and Todd

D. Still, assisted by Jeanette M. Hagen (Downers Grove, Ill.: IVP, 2016), 307.

4   In Chesterton's famous work entitled *Orthodoxy* (New York: MacMillan, 1918), 25.

5   From G. K. Chesterton, *The Thing: Why I Am a Catholic* (New York: MacMillan, 1929), 78.

6   C. S. Lewis, "The Funeral of a Great Myth," in *Christian Reflections* (Grand Rapids: Eerdmans, 1967), 83, 85, 86.

7   Letter to John Beversluis, July 3, 1963, included in *The Collected Letters of C.S. Lewis*, ed. Walter Hooper, 3 vols. (San Francisco: HarperSanFrancisco, 2007), 3:1436–37.

8   In his brief but in-depth study of the matter, *C. S. Lewis on Scripture* (Nashville: Abingdon, 1979), Michael Christensen concludes, "The Bible for him was human literature divinely inspired and authoritative, but not verbally inspired or without error" (11). He is right that Lewis views the Bible through the lens of his great knowledge of great literature, but again, the Bible is not merely great literature, and the inspiration referred to in 2 Tim 3.16 pertains to all the words in Scripture, not just the main ideas.

9   C. S. Lewis, *Reflections on the Psalms* (San Diego: Harcourt, 1986), 111–12.

10   Lewis, *Reflections on the Psalms*, 116.

11   C. S. Lewis, "Modern Translations," in *God in the Dock* (Grand Rapids: Eerdmans, 1970), 230.

12   David Williams, "Surprised by Jack: C. S. Lewis on *Mere Christianity*, the Bible, and Evolutionary Science," *BioLogos*, December 10, 2012, https://biologos.org/articles/surprised-by-jack -c-s-lewis-on-mere-christianity-the-bible-and-evolutionary -science (emphasis original).

13   Williams, "Surprised by Jack" (emphasis original), quoting John G. West, "Darwin in the Dock," in *The Magician's Twin: C. S. Lewis on Science, Scientism, and Society* (Seattle: Discovery Institute Press, 2012).

14 Williams, "Surprised by Jack" (emphasis original), quoting Lewis, *The Problem of Pain*.

15 But not only Paul; see 4 Ezra 3.21–22.

16 On all of this, see my dialogue and critique of the recent works by William Lane Craig (*In Quest of the Historical Adam* [Grand Rapids: Eerdmans, 2021]) and Joshua Swamidass (*The Genealogical Adam and Eve* [Downers Grove, Ill.: IVP, 2021]) on my blog *The Bible and Culture* on Patheos.

17 See the details in Klaus Schmidt's *Sie bauten die ersten Tempel* (Munich: C. H. Beck, 2016).

18 See, rightly, Christensen, *C. S. Lewis on Scripture*, 90.

19 On this whole subject, see Christensen, *C. S. Lewis on Scripture*, 81–91. One of the odder things about some very conservative defenses of Scripture, particularly Reformed ones, is that they reflect not the narrative way of thinking we find in the Bible, where one does one's theologizing out of the fundamental stories, but rather they reflect the Enlightenment tendencies to reduce everything to abstract propositions.

6 THE MODERN QUADRILATERAL, INERRANCY, AND THE OVERRULING OF SCRIPTURE

1 N. T. Wright, *History and Eschatology: Jesus and the Promise of Natural Theology* (Waco: Baylor University Press, 2019), 234.

2 To which I would add that even the most secular of scientists today do indeed operate on some basic faith presuppositions, for example: (1) there is a world outside of the human mind that is knowable through human exploration and inquiry, and (2) the human senses are mostly reliable in conveying accurate information about the outside world to a human being who studies that world. On David Wilkinson, see his *Science, Religion, and the Search for Extraterrestrial Intelligence* (Oxford: Oxford University Press, 2013).

3 Wright, *History and Eschatology*, 12 (emphasis original).

4   Wright, *History and Eschatology*, 21.

5   Wright, *History and Eschatology*, 38.

6   Wright, *History and Eschatology*, 45.

7   Wright, *History and Eschatology*, 47.

8   See my *Jesus, Paul, and the End of the World* (Downers Grove, Ill.: IVP, 1992).

9   See R. Bauckham, *Jesus and the Eyewitnesses*, 2nd ed. (Grand Rapids: Eerdmans, 2017); and also my colleague Craig S. Keener's *Christobiography* (Grand Rapids: Eerdmans, 2019).

10 Wright, *History and Eschatology*, 63.

11 See Karl R. Popper, *The Logic of Scientific Discovery*, 3rd ed. (London: Hutchinson, 1968).

12 Wright, *History and Eschatology*, 111.

13 Wright, *History and Eschatology*, 111 (emphasis original).

14 Wright, *History and Eschatology*, 116.

15 Wright, *History and Eschatology*, 119 (emphasis original).

16 Wright, *History and Eschatology*, 121 (emphasis original).

17 Wright, *History and Eschatology*, 122.

18 Wright, *History and Eschatology*, 130.

19 Wright, *History and Eschatology*, 254 (emphasis original).

20 Wright, *History and Eschatology*, 267.

21 This is found on my blog, *The Bible and Culture*, from November 9–14, 2019, https://www.patheos.com/blogs/bibleandculture.

22 John Wesley, *John Wesley*, ed. Albert C. Outler (Oxford: Oxford University Press, 1964), iv. W. S. Gunter, ed., *Wesley and the Quadrilateral: Renewing the Conversation* (Nashville: Abingdon, 1997).

23 *The United Methodist Church Book of Discipline* (Nashville: Abingdon, 2004), 77.

24 John Wesley, *The Works of John Wesley*, vol. 6, ed. Thomas Jackson (Wesleyan Methodist Book Room, 1872), 354.

25 See further the discussion at "Wesleyan Quadrilateral," Wikipedia, last edited on January 10, 2023, https://en.wikipedia.org/wiki/Wesleyan_Quadrilateral.

26 Ironically, it was often these very conservative and Evangelical churches that were early adopters of the popular-style music services, which contributed to biblical literacy declining in these very churches. But there were other factors as well, for instance, taking a consumer approach to worship—giving the people what they enjoyed and found entertaining, not what God desired and required. There were increasing numbers of young pastors who were not seminary trained, or really biblically literate, never mind knowledgeable about biblical languages and reading good commentaries, who would cook up sermons on popular cultural topics, complete with entertaining stories and anecdotes. None of this increased biblical literacy in the church in the 1980s, nor has it into the present.

27 The Chicago Statement on Biblical Inerrancy, https://www.etsjets.org/files/documents/Chicago_Statement.pdf.

28 Notice, for example, how the psalmist talks about "the thoughts of my heart" or "create in me a clean heart" (e.g., Ps 51) because the assumption is that the heart is the control center of the human person—the center of thoughts, feelings, will. Today, of course, we know the human heart is just a pump. The Bible reflects the assumptions of that era on such matters, but it is not teaching biology.

29 In some ways the Lausanne Covenant statement is more nuanced: "We affirm the divine inspiration, truthfulness and authority of both Old and New Testament Scriptures in their entirety as the only written word of God, without error in all that it affirms, and the only infallible rule of faith and practice." I take "affirmed" to mean "teaches." The Lausanne Covenant statement with commentary by John Stott was first drafted in 1974 and so came before the longer and more famous statement in Chicago, but the Lausanne Covenant was not singularly focused on the Bible and its authority in the way the Chicago Statement is. For the

Lausanne statement on the Bible, see https://lausanne.org/content/lop/lop-3#2.

30 See also the statement at "Inerrancy Quotes," Defending Inerrancy, https://defendinginerrancy.com/inerrancy-quotes/. Once again, a statement almost exclusively made by white males, no women or Arminians listed. Notice the purpose statement on the website, which bears the date 2023: "The Defending Inerrancy initiative was founded by concerned scholars to combat the erosion of biblical inerrancy within the Evangelical community."

31 On which see Ben Witherington III, "The Anti-feminist Tendencies of the Western Text of Acts," *Journal of Biblical Literature* 103, no. 1 (1984): 82–84.

32 On this whole matter, see Ben Witherington III, *Invitation to the New Testament*, 2nd ed. (Oxford: Oxford University Press, 2017). It should also be noted that we owe the chapter divisions that we still use today to Archbishop Langton of Canterbury (1150–1228). There is nothing inspired about them; in fact, some of them are just wrong. For example, Heb 12.1–3, where we find the discussion of Christ as the pioneer and perfector of faith, really belongs in Heb 11, the so-called Hall of Faith chapter.

33 It is, however, telling that X and Y chromosomes do not support the notion that people are "born" a certain way that could involve same-sex predeterminism. They are binary—one is either born male or female. As Francis Collins has said (see the appendix to *The Language of God* [New York: Free Press, 2006]), no one is hardwired in a same-sex way at the level of chromosomes or genetics, unless one is talking about rare genetic abnormalities. The search for a "gay" gene has turned up nothing thus far.

7 *QUO VADIS?*

1 On which see pp. 17–20 above.

2   Contra the claim in Don Kistler, ed., *Sola Scriptura! The Prot-
    estant Position on the Bible* (Sanford, Fla.: Ligonier Ministries,
    2009).

3   Besides the discussion in previous chapters above, con-
    sider, for example, the book of Jude v. 9, which includes
    the following noncanonical sources and ideas: "But even the
    archangel Michael, when he was disputing with the devil
    about the body of Moses, did not himself dare to condemn
    him for slander but said, 'The Lord rebuke you!'" (from the
    Testament of Moses); and then vv. 14–15: "Enoch, the sev-
    enth from Adam, prophesied about them: 'See, the Lord is
    coming with thousands upon thousands of his holy ones to
    judge everyone, and to convict all of them of all the ungodly
    acts they have committed in their ungodliness, and of all
    the defiant words ungodly sinners have spoken against him'"
    (from 1 Enoch); and we could cite other examples from the
    speech of Stephen in Acts 7. This is hardly surprising since
    early Jews, including early Jewish Christians, valued vari-
    ous noncanonical traditions and believed some of them had
    some authority because they told the truth about something.

4   See Henri de Lubac, *Scripture in the Tradition: Milestones in
    Catholic Theology* (Chestnut Ridge, Pa.: Crossroad Publish-
    ing, 2001), on the interpretation of that statement. Perhaps
    more importantly, see also now the 2008 joint Methodist-
    Catholic statement, "Heaven and Earth Are Full of Your
    Glory: A United Methodist and Roman Catholic State-
    ment on the Eucharist and Ecology," United States Confer-
    ence of Catholic Bishops, https://www.usccb.org/resources/
    heaven-and-earth-are-full-your-glory-united-methodist
    -and-roman-catholic-statement. Such joint statements have
    been happening since Vatican II.

5   W. Robert Godfrey, "What Do We Mean by *Sola Scrip-
    tura*?" in *Sola Scriptura! The Protestant Position on the Bible*, ed.
    Don Kistler (Sanford, Fla.: Ligonier Ministries, 2009), 2. As an

194
Notes to Pages 148–156

emeritus professor of church history at a seminary in California, he should have known better than to make false polemical statements like this.

6   Godfrey, "What Do We Mean by *Sola Scriptura*?" 11.

7   See the citation and discussion by W. H. Hutton in *The Cambridge Medieval History*, vol. 2, *The Rise of the Saracens and the Foundation of the Western Empire* (New York: Macmillan, 1913), 247. Godfrey cites this on p. 9 of his article.

8   It is interesting however that christological orthodoxy was recognized and partially settled before there was a canon of the NT. The Council of Nicaea took place in 325 A.D., some forty years before there were clear or final statements about the limits of the NT canon.

9   On all this, see my critique of the recent book *Five Views of the New Testament Canon*, ed. Stanley E. Porter and Benjamin P. Laird (Grand Rapids: Kregel Academic, 2022), on my blog, *The Bible and Culture*, for January 7, 2023, https://www.patheos.com/blogs/bibleandculture.

10 Godfrey, "What Do We Mean by *Sola Scriptura*?" 12.

11 See James White, "*Sola Scriptura* and the Early Church," in Kistler, *Sola Scriptura!* 27, citing Cyril of Jerusalem, *Catechetical Lectures* 4.17.

12 See White, "*Sola Scriptura* and the Early Church."

13 See Ben Witherington III, *The Problem with Evangelical Theology*, 2nd ed. (Waco: Baylor University Press, 2015).

14 This essay on Peter in Rome is one of the last things Lightfoot wrote before his untimely death. It is found in the appendix to his volume *The Apostolic Fathers*, part 1.2 (London: Macmillan, 1890), 501–2.

15 See the last volume that Todd Still and I edited of Lightfoot's unpublished works, *The Epistles of 2 Corinthians and 1 Peter* (Downers Grove, Ill.: IVP, 2016), 193–282.

16 White, "*Sola Scriptura* and the Early Church," 30–32.

17 In S. B. Ferguson's helpful essay "Scripture and Tradition," in Kistler, *Sola Scriptura!* 91–110, here 96–103.

18 On biblical theology and hermeneutics that do justice to the historical nature of the biblical texts and progressive revelation found in them, see my *Biblical Theology: The Convergence of the Canon* (Cambridge: Cambridge University Press, 2020). As I stress there, biblical theology, theology that can actually be found in the Bible or is clearly entailed by the Bible, is one thing; later historical theologies and systematic theologies that all too often are guilty of the sin of anachronism are another thing. Clyde Kilby once said, "The Bible comes to us not as systematic theology but as great literature" (in Michael Christensen, *C. S. Lewis on Scripture* [Nashville: Abingdon, 1979], 10). He's right about what he denies, but the Bible is not just great literature; it makes truth claims on history and on us beyond those of great literature. You would hope that the most strident advocates of *sola Scriptura* and inerrancy would recognize the difference between biblical theology and later Catholic, Protestant, or Orthodox theologies not necessarily stated or clearly implied by the Bible.

19 See the detailed discussion of this in Ben Witherington III, *Letters and Homilies for Hellenized Christians*, vol. 1, *A Socio-rhetorical Commentary on Titus, 1–2 Timothy and 1–3 John* (Downers Grove, Ill.: IVP, 2006), 23–38.

Select Bibliography

Abraham, William J. *The Bible: Beyond the Impasse*. Dallas: Highland Loch Press, 2012.

———. "The Future of Scripture: In Search of a Theology of Scripture." *Wesleyan Theological Journal* 46, no. 2 (2011): 13.

Adams, Craig L. "What John Wesley Actually Said about the Bible." 2012. http://www.craigladams.com/archive/files/john -wesley-on-the-bible.html.

Baker, Ken. "The Puritans and the Bible." November 16, 2007. https://kenbaker.wordpress.com/2007/11/16/the-puritans -and-the-bible/.

Barrett, C. K. "The First New Testament." *Novum Testamentum* 38 (1996): 94–104.

Bauckham, R. *Jesus and the Eyewitnesses*. 2nd ed. Grand Rapids: Eerdmans, 2017.

Bingham, Jeffrey. "Senses of Scripture in the Second Century: Irenaeus, Scripture, and Noncanonical Christian Texts." *Journal of Religion* 97, no. 1 (2017). Accessed December 24, 2022. https:// www.journals.uchicago.edu/doi/10.1086/688994.

Blowers, P. M. *The Bible in Greek Christian Antiquity*. Notre Dame, Ind.: University of Notre Dame Press, 1997.

Bradshaw, William. "English Puritanism." In *Several Treatises of Worship & Ceremonies*. London, 1660.

Cameron, Euan, ed. *The New Cambridge History of the Bible*. Vol. 3, *From 1450–1750*. Cambridge: Cambridge University Press, 2016.

Cartwright, Thomas. *A Directory of Church-government. . . Found in the study of the most accomplished Divine, Mr. Thomas Cartwright, after his decease; and reserved to be published for such a time as this*. London: Printed for John Wright in the Old-baily, 1644.

Chesterton, G. K. *Orthodoxy*. New York: MacMillan, 1918.

———. *The Thing: Why I Am a Catholic*. New York: MacMillan, 1929.

"The Chicago Statement on Biblical Inerrancy." 1978. https://www.etsjets.org/files/documents/Chicago_Statement.pdf.

Christensen, Michael. *C. S. Lewis on Scripture*. Nashville: Abingdon, 1979.

Collins, Francis. *The Language of God*. New York: Free Press, 2006.

Craig, William Lane. *In Quest of the Historical Adam*. Grand Rapids: Eerdmans, 2021.

de Lubac, Henri. *Scripture in the Tradition: Milestones in Catholic Theology*. Chestnut Ridge, Pa.: Crossroad Publishing, 2001.

Dornfeld, Hope V. "A Man of One Book: John Wesley's Theology of Scripture." *Diligence: Journal of the Liberty University Online Religion Capstone in Research and Scholarship* 3 (2019), article 2. https://digitalcommons.liberty.edu/djrc/vol3/iss1/2.

Edwards, Rem B. "John Wesley's Non-literal Literalism and Hermeneutics of Love." *Wesleyan Theological Journal* 51, no. 2 (2016): 26–40. https://philarchive.org/archive/EDWQWN.

Ehrman, Bart. *Lost Christianities: The Battle for Scripture and the Faiths We Never Knew*. Oxford: Oxford University Press, 2003.

Epp, E. J. "Critical Editions of the New Testament, and the Development of Text-Critical Methods: From Erasmus to Griesbach (1516–1807)." In *The New Cambridge History of the Bible*, vol. 3, *From 1450–1750*, edited by Euan Cameron, 110–37. Cambridge: Cambridge University Press, 2016.

Eusebius. *Church History, Life of Constantine the Great, and Oration in Praise of Constantine*. In vol. 1 of *The Nicene and Post-Nicene Fathers*, second series. Edited by Philip Schaff and Henry Wace. New York: Christian Literature Company, 1890.

Ferguson, S. B. "Scripture and Tradition." In *Sola Scriptura! The Protestant Position on the Bible*, edited by Don Kistler, 91–110. Sanford, Fla.: Ligonier Ministries, 2009.

Gamble, Harry. "Marcion and the Canon." In *The Cambridge History of Christianity*, vol. 1, *Origins to Constantine*, edited by Margaret M. Mitchell and Frances M. Young, 195–213. Cambridge: Cambridge University Press, 2006.

Geisler, Norman. "Irenaeus on Scripture and Tradition." 2014. https://normangeisler.com/irenaeus-tradition-scripture/.

Godfrey, W. Robert. "What Do We Mean by *Sola Scriptura*?" In *Sola Scriptura! The Protestant Position on the Bible*, edited by Don Kistler, 1–26. Sanford, Fla.: Ligonier Ministries, 2009.

Greenwood, John. *The Writings of John Greenwood, 1587–1590*. Edited by Leland H. Carlson. London: George Allen and Unwin, 1962.

Guarini, Battista. "A Program of Teaching and Learning." In *Humanist Educational Treatises*, edited and translated by Craig W. Kallendorf, 260–309. Cambridge, Mass.: Harvard University Press, 2002.

Guinot, Jean-Noël. "Theodoret of Cyrus: Bishop and Exegete." In *The Bible in Greek Christian Antiquity*, edited by P. M. Blowers, 163–93. Notre Dame, Ind.: University of Notre Dame Press, 1997.

Gunter, W. S., ed. *Wesley and the Quadrilateral: Renewing the Conversation*. Nashville: Abingdon, 1997.

Hahneman, Geoffrey M. *The Muratorian Fragment and the Development of the Canon*. Oxford: Clarendon, 1992.

Hayward, C. T. R. "Scripture in the Jerusalem Temple." In *The New Cambridge History of the Bible*, vol. 1, *From the Beginnings to 600*, edited by J. C. Paget and J. Schaper, 321–44. Cambridge: Cambridge University Press, 2013.

Heine, Ronald. "Reading the Bible with Origen." In *The Bible in Greek Christian Antiquity*, edited by P. M. Blowers, 131–48. Notre Dame, Ind.: University of Notre Dame Press, 1997.

Hengel, M. *The Septuagint as Christian Scripture*. Grand Rapids: Baker Academic, 2004.

Hutton, W. H., ed. *The Cambridge Medieval History*. Vol. 2, *The Rise of the Saracens and the Foundation of the Western Empire*. New York: Macmillan, 1913.

John Chrysostom. *Homilies on Genesis 18–45*. Translated by Robert C. Hill. Catholic University of America Press, 2001.

———. *The Homilies of S. John Chrysostom, Archbishop of Constantinople, on the Gospel of St. John*. Oxford: John Henry Parker, 1848–1852.

———. *The Homilies of S. John Chrysostom, Archbishop of Constantinople, on the epistle of S. Paul the Apostle to the Romans*. 3rd ed. with rev. translation. Oxford: James Parker, 1877.

———. *The homilies of S. John Chrysostom on the second epistle of St. Paul the apostle to the Corinthians*. Translated with notes and indices by Charles Marriott and John Ashworth. Oxford: John Henry Parker, 1848.

Jones, Scott. *John Wesley's Conception and Use of Scripture*. Nashville: Kingswood Books, 1995.

Josephus. *Jewish Antiquities, Volume IX: Book 20*. Translated by Louis H. Feldman. Loeb Classical Library 456. Cambridge, Mass.: Harvard University Press, 1965.

Jourjon, M. "Irenaeus's Reading of the Bible." In *The Bible in Greek Christian Antiquity*, edited by P. M. Blowers, 105–11. Notre Dame, Ind.: University of Notre Dame Press, 1997.

Judge, E. A. *Social Distinctives of the Christians in the First Century*. Edited by David Scholer. Grand Rapids: Baker Academic, 2007.

Keener, Craig S. *Christobiography*. Grand Rapids: Eerdmans, 2019.

Kistler, Don, ed. *Sola Scriptura! The Protestant Position on the Bible*. Sanford, Fla.: Ligonier Ministries, 2009.

Kraye, Jill. "The Revival of Greek Studies in the West." In *The New Cambridge History of the Bible*, vol. 3, *From 1450–1750*, edited by Euan Cameron, 37–60. Cambridge: Cambridge University Press, 2016.

Lamarche, Paul. "The Septuagint: The Bible of the Earliest Christians." In *The Bible in Greek Christian Antiquity*, edited by P. M. Blowers, 15–29. Notre Dame, Ind.: University of Notre Dame Press, 1997.

Lewis, C. S. *The Collected Letters of C.S. Lewis*. Edited by Walter Hooper. 3 vols. San Francisco: HarperSanFrancisco, 2007.

———. "The Funeral of a Great Myth." In *Christian Reflections*. Grand Rapids: Eerdmans, 1967.

———. "Modern Translations." In *God in the Dock*. Grand Rapids: Eerdmans, 1970.

———. *Reflections on the Psalms*. San Diego: Harcourt, 1986.

Lightfoot, J. B. *The Acts of the Apostles: A Newly Discovered Commentary*. Edited by Ben Witherington III and Todd D. Still. Assisted by Jeanette M. Hagen. Downers Grove, Ill.: IVP, 2014.

———. *The Apostolic Fathers*. Part 1.2. London: Macmillan, 1890.

———. *The Epistles of 2 Corinthians and 1 Peter: Newly Discovered Commentaries*. Edited by Ben Witherington III and Todd D. Still. Assisted by Jeanette M. Hagen. Downers Grove, Ill.: IVP, 2016.

Luther, Martin. *Luther's Works*. Volume 32, *Career of the Reformer, Part II*. Edited by George W. Forell. Philadelphia: Muhlenberg Press, 1958.

MacDonald, Lee. *The Biblical Canon: Its Origin, Transmission, and Authority*. 2nd ed. Grand Rapids: Baker, 2006.

Maddox, Randy. *Rethinking Wesley's Theology for Contemporary Methodism*. Nashville: Kingswood Books, 1998.

———. "The Rule of Christian Faith, Practice, and Hope: John Wesley on the Bible." *Methodist Review* 3 (2011): 1–35. https://methodistreview.org/index.php/mr/article/view/45/68.

McGrath, Alister. *In the Beginning: The Story of the King James Bible*. New York: Doubleday, 2001.

Metzger, Bruce M. *The Canon of the New Testament: Its Origin, Development, and Significance*. Oxford: Clarendon, 1997.

Minns, D. "Truth and Tradition: Irenaeus." In *The Cambridge History of Christianity*, vol. 1, *Origins to Constantine*, edited by Margaret M. Mitchell and Frances M. Young, 261–73. Cambridge: Cambridge University Press, 2006.

Mitchell, Margaret M. "The Emergence of the Written Record." In *The Cambridge History of Christianity*, vol. 1, *Origins to Constantine*, edited by Margaret M. Mitchell and Frances M. Young, 177–94. Cambridge: Cambridge University Press, 2006.

———. *The Heavenly Trumpet*. Louisville: Westminster John Knox, 2002.

Nock, A. D. *Conversion*. Baltimore: Johns Hopkins University Press, 1998.

Outler, Albert C., ed. *John Wesley*. Oxford: Oxford University Press, 1964.

Perkins, William. *The Work of William Perkins*. Introduced and edited by Ian Breward. 3 vols. The Courtenay Library of Reformation Classics. Sutton Berkshire: Courtenay Press, 1970.

Pettegree, Andrew. *Brand Luther: 1517, Printing and the Making of the Reformation*. New York: Penguin, 2005.

Popper, Karl R. *The Logic of Scientific Discovery*. 3rd ed. London: Hutchinson, 1968.

Rex, Richard. "Humanist Bible Controversies." In *The New Cambridge History of the Bible*, vol. 3, *From 1450–1750*, edited by Euan Cameron, 61–81. Cambridge: Cambridge University Press, 2016.

Schaff, Philip. *History of the Christian Church*. Vol. 6, *The Middle Ages, A.D. 1294–1517*. New York: Scribner's, 1910; repr., Grand Rapids: Eerdmans, 1980.

———. "Luther's Translation of the Bible." In *History of the Christian Church*, vol. 7, 340–54. New York: Charles Scribner's Sons, 1910.

Schmidt, Klaus. *Sie bauten die ersten Tempel*. Munich: C. H. Beck, 2016.

Stark, Rodney. *The Rise of Christianity*. Princeton: Princeton University Press, 1996.

Still, Todd D., and David E. Wilhite, eds. *Tertullian and Paul*. New York: Bloomsbury, 2013.

Swamidass, Joshua. *The Genealogical Adam and Eve*. Downers Grove, Ill.: IVP, 2021.

Trebilco, Paul R. *Outsider Designations and Boundary Construction in the New Testament*. Cambridge: Cambridge University Press, 2021.

Treloar, G. R. *Lightfoot the Historian*. Tübingen: Mohr Siebeck, 1998.

The United Methodist Church Book of Discipline. Nashville: Abingdon, 2004.

Valla, Lorenzo. *Collatio Novi Testamenti*. Edited by A. Perosa. Florence: Sansoni, 1970.

———. *On the Donation of Constantine*. Translated by G. W. Bowersock. I Tatti Renaissance Library 24. Cambridge: Harvard University Press, 2007.

———. *Opera Omnia*. Edited by E. Garin. 2 vols. Turin: Bottega d'Erasmo, 1962.

van Campenhausen, H. *The Formation of the Christian Bible*. Philadelphia: Fortress, 1972.

Wagner, J. Ross. *Herald of the Good News: Isaiah and Paul in Concert in the Letter to the Romans*. Leiden: Brill, 2000.

———. *Reading the Sealed Book: Old Greek Isaiah and the Problem of Septuagint Hermeneutics*. Tübingen: Mohr Siebeck, 2013.

Wesley, John. *Explanatory Notes upon the New Testament*. 3rd American ed. New York: D. Hitt and T. Ware, 1812.

———. *John Wesley*. Edited by Albert C. Outler. Oxford: Oxford University Press, 1964.

———. *The Letters of John Wesley*. Edited by John Telford. 8 vols. London: Epworth, 1960.

———. *Sermons on Several Occasions*. 2 vols. 11th ed. London: William Tegg and Co., 1853.

———. *Wesley's Standard Sermons*. 2 vols. Edited by Edward H. Sugden. London: Epworth Press, 1961.

———. *The Works of John Wesley*. Volume 6. Edited by Thomas Jackson. Wesleyan Methodist Book Room, 1872.

———. *The Works of John Wesley*. Volume 22, *Journal and Diaries V (1765–75)*. Edited by W. Reginald Ward and Richard P. Heitzenrater. Abingdon: Nashville, 1993.

———. *The Works of John Wesley*. Volume 23, *Journal and Diaries VI (1776–86)*. Edited by W. Reginald Ward and Richard P. Heitzenrater. Abingdon: Nashville, 1995.

———. *The Works of the Rev. John Wesley*. London: Printed at the Conference-Office, 1812.

White, James. "*Sola Scriptura* and the Early Church." In *Sola Scriptura! The Protestant Position on the Bible*, edited by Don Kistler, 27–38. Sanford, Fla.: Ligonier Ministries, 2009.

Wilkinson, David. *Science, Religion, and the Search for Extraterrestrial Intelligence*. Oxford: Oxford University Press, 2013.

Williams, David. "Surprised by Jack: C. S. Lewis on *Mere Christianity*, the Bible, and Evolutionary Science." *BioLogos*, December 10, 2012. https://biologos.org/articles/surprised-by-jack-c-s-lewis-on-mere-christianity-the-bible-and-evolutionary-science.

Wilson, A. N. *C. S. Lewis: A Biography*. New York: Norton, 1990.

Wilson, Luke. "How Polycarp (and Others) Show the Early Use of the New Testament." The Sacred Faith. Updated November 21, 2021. https://www.thatancientfaith.uk/home/perma/1637485200/article/polycarp-show-the-early-use-of-the-new-testament.html.

Witherington, Ben, III. "The Anti-feminist Tendencies of the Western Text of Acts." *Journal of Biblical Literature* 103, no. 1 (1984): 82–84.

———. *Biblical Theology: The Convergence of the Canon*. Cambridge: Cambridge University Press, 2020.

———. *Invitation to the New Testament*. 2nd ed. Oxford: Oxford University Press, 2017.

———. *Jesus, Paul, and the End of the World*. Downers Grove, Ill.: IVP, 1992.

———. *John's Wisdom*. Louisville: Westminster John Knox, 1995.

———. *Letters and Homilies for Hellenized Christians*. Vol. 1, *A Socio-rhetorical Commentary on Titus, 1–2 Timothy and 1–3 John*. Downers Grove, Ill.: IVP, 2006.

———. *The Living Word of God*. Waco: Baylor University Press, 2020.

———. *The Problem with Evangelical Theology*. 2nd ed. Waco: Baylor University Press, 2015.

———. "Sola Scriptura and the Reformation." *Journal of the Evangelical Theological Society* 60, no. 4 (2017): 817–28.

———. "The Turn of the Christian Era: The Tale of Dionysius Exeguus." *Biblical Archaeology Review* 43, no. 6 (2017): 26. https://www.baslibrary.org/biblical-archaeology-review/43/6/8.

———. *What's in the Word*. Waco: Baylor University Press, 2009.

Witherington, Ben, III, and Jason A. Myers. *New Testament Rhetoric*. 2nd exp. ed. Eugene, Ore.: Cascade, 2022.

Wright, N. T. *History and Eschatology: Jesus and the Promise of Natural Theology*. Waco: Baylor University Press, 2019.

Index of Subjects

ad fontes, 40, 98
analogia fidei, analogy of faith, 65, 79
Anglican, Anglicanism, 56, 61–64, 68, 71, 145, 157, 186n20
Apocrypha, apocryphal, 53–54, 56, 63, 70, 80, 97, 184n9, 185n13
Apostle, 10, 13, 15, 17–21, 24, 26, 53, 63, 67, 73, 97, 145, 154–55, 177n26; Apostle's Creed, 65, 81, 183n1; apostolic, 7, 12–16, 20, 153–55, 159, 184n7; Apostolic Fathers, 11–12; apostolicity, 177n26
applicability of the Bible, 126, 136
Aquinas, 33, 37, 44, 117
Athanasius, 156, 160

Augustine, 25, 36, 152
authority, final, xi, xiii, 2–3, 12, 29, 30, 32, 34, 37, 47, 74, 86, 98, 105–6, 117, 123, 126, 139, 141–42, 144–45, 148, 150–51, 155–57, 159–61, 184n9; main, 117, 159
autographs, 69, 130, 133–35, 139

Calvin, John, 32, 38, 57, 59, 61–62, 68, 70, 144; Calvinistic, Calvinism, 57, 88–89, 158, 186n20
canon, canonical, 11, 16, 18, 26, 28, 34, 58, 63, 71, 80, 98, 152, 177n26, 179n2, 182n16, 185n13; canon within the canon, 84; canonical Gospels, 13; canonizing, canonization, xi, 17, 22; deuterocanonical, 16, 20,

priest, 3, 8, 31–32, 34–35, 38,
    66–67, 71, 147, 160–61,
    176n18; priesthood, 66–67
prima Scriptura, 26, 105–6
prophet, prophetic, xii, 2–3,
    17–19, 24, 26, 63, 73, 75,
    114, 147, 173n3, 187n23; the
    Prophets, 3, 15, 29, 59
Protestant, Protestantism,
    xi–xiii, 41, 47–48, 56–57,
    59, 66–71, 74, 85, 89,
    97–98, 105, 132, 136, 139,
    144–50, 152, 156–57, 159,
    180n5, 182n16, 184n9,
    193n2, 195n18; Bible, 70, 97
Puritan, Puritanism, 61–65,
    67–68, 71

Quadrilateral, 109, 123–24, 126

reason, reasoning, reasonable,
    xi, 29, 61, 85–88, 107,
    121–26, 144, 153, 161;
    rational, rationalism, 97,
    117–18
Reformation, xii, 7, 29, 34–35,
    41, 50–52, 89, 97, 111, 144,
    146, 160; English, 39, 61,
    70, 145; German, xi, 39,
    57–59, 70, 144, 152, 159;
    Protestant, 41, 183n6;
    Swiss, 39, 47, 70, 144, 152
Reformed, 62, 67, 71, 74, 89,
    136, 145–46, 158, 189n19

revelation, 6, 25, 96, 100, 121,
    128–29, 157, 186n23, 195n18
Rule of Faith, 81, 191n29

salvation, salvific, 8–9, 11,
    37, 59, 63–66, 72, 75–76,
    79, 86–87, 100–101, 124,
    133, 135, 137, 146–48,
    153, 157–59, 161, 165;
    soteriology, 124, 147
science, scientific, scientist,
    xii, 83–84, 86, 89, 91–97,
    99, 100, 102, 109, 111, 130,
    134–35, 158, 189n2
scribe, 10, 37; transcribe,
    transcriber, 28, 139
Scriptures, xi, 2, 11, 14–15,
    18–24, 26–28, 33–34,
    36–38, 47, 63, 65, 73–76,
    81, 87, 95, 98, 101, 121, 123,
    125, 128–29, 132, 136–37,
    144–45, 148, 153, 159, 161,
    181n11, 185n13; Hebrew,
    OT, 3–4, 10, 15, 21, 191n29;
    NT, 21, 191n29
Septuagint (LXX), 5–7, 20,
    45, 68–69, 83, 98, 174n11,
    179n2, 182n16, 184n9
sola fide, 49, 76
sola Scriptura, xi–xii, 26–27,
    29, 32, 34–35, 39, 51, 58, 62,
    67, 69, 71, 85–87, 89–99,
    105, 126, 133, 142–46, 153,

Index of Scripture and Ancient Sources